To

Mr. Vanderbilt Webb

Who in the Third Crisis of our Nation's Life has given moral and financial support to preserve our form of government and has thus proved worthy of the heroic men and women who founded the Republic.

With the grateful appreciation of the National Committee to Uphold Constitutional Government.

Samuel B. Pettengill,
Chairman

June
1940

SMOKE-SCREEN

Smoke-Screen

By

SAMUEL B. PETTENGILL
Former member of Congress (Indiana)

Author of

JEFFERSON, THE FORGOTTEN MAN
HOT OIL

Southern Publishers, Inc.

NEW YORK   CHICAGO
KINGSPORT, TENNESSEE

To

J. H. P.

FOREWORD

THIS BOOK is written to demonstrate that we are moving *toward* National Socialism, and that from now on, we should move *away* from it.

It is not intended as a partisan discussion. It is, however, political in the sense that the American Constitution is political. Heretofore, both great parties and their leaders and platforms have been forthright in their loyalty to the fundamental concepts of government upon which we have built the greatest and happiest civilization the world has ever known.

To the men and women of both parties who still think that America is "the last best hope of earth," and are willing to fight to save it for their boys and girls, I dedicate these pages.

To Republicans I recall Abraham Lincoln's words: "The principles of Jefferson are the definitions and axioms of a free society."

To Democrats, of whom I have been one for a lifetime, I recall Jefferson's admonition, "What has destroyed liberty and the rights of man in every government which has existed under the sun? The generalizing and concentrating all powers into one body."

To those who have grown weary of our great effort to be free, and have embraced, whatever the label or disguise or excuse, the principles of Karl Marx, and are willing to become the pawns of the State, I recall President Roosevelt's words in 1936, "We have built up new instruments of public power". . . which in other hands . . . "would provide shackles for the liberties of the people."

If, after full debate, the American people were to deliberately and freely select National Socialism as a way of life by the democratic process of ascertaining the major voice of all the people, no one could question their right to do so, however mistaken we would consider their decision.

But after eight years in Congress I am certain that the American people have not chosen that course, and I do not think they will *freely* and *deliberately* make that decision.

The decision is being made for them behind the "smoke-screen" of an unguaranteed political promise of the more abundant life which our great age is capable of producing. Hence the title of this book, "Smoke-Screen."

The single important question is whether the general welfare we all seek can be more certainly attained under free enterprise or collectivism; under the Constitution of the United States which makes the State the servant of the people, or under Marxism, which makes the people the slaves of the State.

To assist in answering that question is my only purpose. For a fuller statement of the argument for "The American Way," I refer the reader to "Jefferson, the Forgotten Man."

SAMUEL B. PETTENGILL

South Bend, Indiana
April 15, 1940

CONTENTS

step by step, and by muffled tread. It will move under the smoke-screen of laudable "objectives" to its hidden goal. That goal is National Socialism.

"It gives us National Socialists a special secret pleasure to see how the people about us are unaware of what is really happening to them," said Adolf Hitler. (*The Voice of Destruction*—Hermann Rauschnig.)

It is not necessary, nor does it do any good, to ascribe unworthy motives to anyone even though they may exist. The truth is that many people, here and abroad, have lost faith in free institutions. They believe that collectivism actually is better for mankind. It certainly better satisfies the egos of those who rule mankind.

I am willing to concede that Hitler, Mussolini, or Stalin believes he is serving his nation. So with those who would control all American business to serve what they conceive to be the good of the State. They, and their idolaters, would resent the term "American Hitler." They prefer the word "humanitarian." But if the purpose and certain result is a Nazi America, will admirable adjectives save us?

Perhaps these leaders—some of them at least—do not see clearly where they are headed. But that others do cannot be doubted—for example, Adolph Berle, Jr., Assistant Secretary of State.

Witness Mr. Berle's statement before the Temporary National Economic Committee. "The government will have to enter into direct financing of activities now supposed to be private, and a *continuance* of that direct financing must be *inevitably* that the government will ultimately *control* and *own* those activities. . . . Over a period of years the government will *gradually* come to *own most of the productive plants of the United States*." This recent and explicit statement is of the same piece as the program of Rexford Guy Tugwell made public seven years ago. They have never been repudiated by the President of the United States.

Another weathervane is Harlow R. Person, consultant for PWA, and Rural Electrification Administration. He says: "The establishment of an expanding social economy will require the elimination and revision of many elemental factors. Let us hope this can be accomplished without blind violence—The new order will require modification of such concepts as those of private property—of the function of the corporation—of saving, spending for investment and consumption. The leaders in Russia have large visions in respect to liberty eventually. It has been restricted while they *are getting their foothold!*"

It is time for Americans—Democratic Americans and Republican Americans—to take their eyes off Russia and the October, 1917, revolution. It is wholly unlikely that we will go that route. We will continue to pay lip service to privately owned property and the profit-motive in place of the bayonet as an incentive to produce. But the control and the profits, if not the actual management of property will be gradually—and stealthily—taken from its owners and gathered into the hands of bureaucrats. For some time we will continue to call it American, but it will become a species of Naziism.

In 1932 we thought the definition of the "New Deal" was the Democratic party platform of that year, one of the best ever written. But the most important political fact in the United States today is that the second or third New Deal is fundamentally fascist. Our attention is diverted at the front door by a permanent "emergency." We stick out our tongues and cry "down with the reds." This gives us a virtuous feeling of patriotism. But while we pay this riskless tribute to our historic past, socialism creeps upon us through the back door unawares.

No follower of Jefferson and no follower of Lincoln is under any obligation of party loyalty to stand mute while this goes on. The goal is the antithesis of all they wrought for. In "Jefferson, The Forgotten Man" I pointed out that the American Revolution was essentially a revolt against a collectivism of the same kidney as the third New Deal. (The 18th Century word was "mercantilism.") We are now asked to embrace the same kind of tyrannies which our forebears crossed the stormy North Atlantic to escape.

Four score and seven years later, at Gettysburg, Abraham Lincoln reflected upon this "new nation conceived in liberty" economic, as much as political and religious. He asked himself and us the sober question "whether *that nation* or *any nation* so conceived and so dedicated *can long endure.*" He spoke of the "great task remaining before us" and asked that "we take increased devotion" to that cause in order that "this nation, under God, shall have a *new birth of freedom.*"

A new birth of freedom! Is it possible that we are finally awakening to the challenge of the returning Caesars?

As the 1940s begin what do we see is being planned for our further salvation?

Mr. Secretary of the Navy Charles Edison proposes that the President be given war powers in peace times, the power to seize factories and railroads, to fix prices and hence to fix wages and regiment labor. It is the same exact quantity and quality of power which Herr Hitler exercises to run the Nazi navy.

Senator Wagner proposes to further invade the field of free enterprise by selling government annuities—a clever and "humanitarian" device by which a spendthrift government could take over the assets of insurance companies and stuff their portfolios with more government bonds. This would undermine the security of some 64,000,000 thrifty people.

A bill is pending to give Mr. Secretary of the Interior Ickes the power to manage the petroleum industry—third largest in the nation.

A bill is pending to socialize the practice of medicine and thus destroy a great profession while lowering our health standards from world leadership to the level of the ordinary pay roller in government.

The United States Forest Service recommends that it be given power to regulate lumbering on all privately owned land. The slogan in Washington is not yet "Blood and Soil," but we are being pushed toward a Nazi America.

The Securities and Exchange Commission tells a great utility company that it can't sell bonds, but must sell stock, thus taking the management away from those who own it, as Hitler does across the sea.

Under power conferred by the reorganization bill of 1939, Mr. Roosevelt forces the resignation of the governor of the Farm Credit Administration and transfers it to Mr. Secretary of Agriculture Wallace. The effect of this is to take a great rural credit agency, independently operated in large part by farmers themselves in which they have invested $130,000,000 in stock, and turn it over to the politicians who farm the farmers.

The Supreme Court holds that it has no power to interfere with decisions of the National Labor Relations Board fixing bargaining units. Consequently, industry wide (which is nation wide) bargaining is permitted, thus destroying local self government in industry, and constituting a long stride toward the "corporative state" of Benito and Adolf.

The federal government, by secret pressures, induces the radio broadcasters to write a code forbidding the purchase of time to discuss controversial questions, and attempts, thereby, to destroy freedom of speech by critics of government policies.

The United States Housing Administration is asking Congress for $800 million more to build "low cost" subsidized housing, indirectly competing with private housing and at the expense of all house owners and all taxpayers.

The Commodity Exchange Administration proposes to bring twelve presently unregulated futures markets under the same supervision as thirteen commodities now under their control. Just as if the whole effort to control the economic life of a great nation is not, in itself, gambling in futures.

The Temporary National Economic Committee is reported to be preparing a "blast against American business beyond comparison with anything in history"—its thesis being that private enterprise is a failure; life insurance a blood sucker; private banking outmoded; and that National Socialism is the hope of the world.

Through cheap money artificially produced by a government that is constantly borrowing billions, the earnings of all savings institutions—banks, insurance companies, building and loan—are shrinking, thus impairing the security for old age of all thrifty people. For example, at four per cent, savings of $12,000 would yield $480 a year, or $40 a month for the "years of the locust." But at $1\frac{1}{4}$ per cent now in force in savings banks in the Chicago area (in New Jersey it is one per cent) it requires $38,400 to yield the same income, a principal sum that is impossible for the average thrifty family to hope to accumulate. In other words, one would have to earn and save $26,400 more in order to receive the same and no more income. At $1\frac{1}{4}$ per cent $12,000 today yields only $150 a year, or $12.50 a month. Contrasted with $40 a month this is a loss to the thrifty Americans of more than 68 per cent. When the thrifty are wiped out, who will defend democracy?[1]

---

[1] Article 17 of the Nazi official program said "we demand the abolition of mortgage interest." (The New Deal in Europe—Emil Lengyel.) Of

A like loss of investment income is undermining all privately endowed hospitals, churches, schools, and colleges. Moreover, as their income shrinks, the income and estates of their benefactors are being shrunk by mounting taxes to support Government. This constitutes a threat to the independence and integrity of these democratic institutions the seriousness of which is only now being realized. Is the Federal treasury to become the receiver in bankruptcy of Christian charity, education and religion?

I.P.M.—or the Industrial Mobilization Plan—now in blue print means totalitarianism on the European model and the blackout of American liberty in the event of war. How much of free institutions would be salvaged in peace? Is it not far more likely that we shall lose our democracy at home than destroy dictatorship abroad?

These are but a few of the plans *now* in the blue print stage, or actively "in the works." It is not likely that many of them will be pressed before the 1940 election is hurdled. But then—what?

The collectivist program already on the books would require a volume to index. It would take months to catalog the thousands of pages of statutes, and tens of thousands of pages of executive orders, administrative regulations and bureaucratic rulings (having the force of law) under which government has been bringing all privately owned business within its iron grasp.

This is not to condemn, out of hand, the whole program. I have slight regard for those who say, either, "I'm 100 (or 1,000) (or 1,000,000) per cent for the New Deal," or "I'm

course that means the socialization of debt. We have not "abolished" interest, but in driving rates paid by savings institutions down to 1¼% we are approaching the zero point.

Interest is a means by which the accumulation of wealth is encouraged. With it the saver may hope to provide for his old age, standing on his own feet, an independent and self respecting citizen. The alternative presented by National Socialism is to make him a pensioner of the state, a return to the "bread and circuses" of the Caesars.

100 per cent against it." Some of the program has been necessary and wholesome, for example, regulation of banking and the sale of blue sky securities, in which there had been such shameful betrayals of public trust.

Liberty under law remains the hope of the world. It is not liberty alone, nor law alone. An excess of liberty is anarchy, from which all men revolt. An excess of law is despotism, from which free men revolt. It is our great task "to combine that degree of liberty, without which law is tyranny, with that degree of law without which liberty becomes license."

To police or regulate a business to such degree as may be necessary in the public interest is as old as Magna Charta. "So use your own as not to injure your neighbor." That is part of the "American Way."

But that thin wavering line between liberty and despotism is surely crossed——

When government ceases to regulate and begins to manage, ceases to be an impartial umpire in the economic game and becomes a player,

When government competes with its citizens in the production of wealth,

When government becomes the untaxed owner of property not necessary for strictly governmental functions,

When government through spending and debt levies a tax tribute on private business that it cannot carry and continue to grow,

When it attempts to control the umpire between Government and people—the courts—either by packing or bringing into disrepute,

When it attempts to use the vast financial power of blank check government, and the prestige of the executive office to purge from Congress undesired representatives of

the people, and to nominate and elect "King's Men" to
public office,

When it attempts to bring the free press of the nation
into public contempt,

When it attempts to control the radio,

When it becomes the active ally of Labor against Investor, or Labor against Labor,

When it attempts to deprive the citizen of effective ap-
peal to the courts from bureaucratic rulings,

When it destroys the individual states and local com-
munities by pre-empting their tax resources, absorbing
their functions and in doing this atrophy the citizen's
sense of responsibility for *his* government, i.e., government
of, for and by the people, which is the beating heart of our
representative democracy,

When it builds up a huge governmental machine which
acquires a "vested right" in public office, and uses its enormous voting power to perpetuate its hold on the public
payroll,

or, generally when it hires personnel who are hostile to
the free enterprise system and actively promote socialistic,
communistic or fascistic knifing of the American Constitution.

It does not answer the question to say that it is hard to
tell when twilight ends and when night begins (that because the government runs the post office as a species of
state socialism, it can with equal logic take over and socialize all business). There is a point *beyond which it is night*.
There is a point beyond which the state is no longer the
Servant of the Citizen but his Master. There is a point
where freedom ends, and despotism begins. There is a
point between Caesar, and God, beyond which Caesar
must not enter.

In succeeding chapters I shall endeavor to summarize the advance of National Socialism by government competition with free enterprise, by excessive bureaucratic regimentation, by excessive taxation, and by the development of the "seamless web" theory, amounting to a profound constitutional change destroying the powers and rights of the States and their people.

I shall then attempt to ask how much have we gained, or lost by this process and finally, because I learned more about petroleum during my service in Congress than any other branch of American industry I shall use it as a case study of the difference in method and result between free enterprise and National Socialism.

2

KARL MARX—IMMIGRANT

KARL MARX had ten "points" in his platform. Point one was: "Centralization of credit in the hands of the State by means of a national bank with state capital and an exclusive monopoly."

Has this program come to America? Let us see. Twenty years ago the Socialist Party of the United States, in its Declaration of Principles said that its purpose *when in power* is "to transfer the ownership of industries to the people, *beginning* with those of a public character, such as *banking, insurance,* mining, transportation and communications."

We come to 1932. Rexford Guy Tugwell said—"Business will logically be required to disappear. This is not an overstatement for the sake of emphasis; *it is literally meant.* . . . National planning implies guidance of capital uses. . . . Capital allocation would depend on knowledge from some planning agency, of how much for a measured future period ought to be put to one use rather than to another. The first step in control would be to limit self-allocation."

Four years later, in 1936, the effort to limit self-allocation of capital funds found expression in the undistributed profits tax. The thought, gentle reader, was that politicians could spend your money much more wisely than you could who had earned and saved it. This experi-

21

ment in National Socialism was a chief contributing factor to the crash of 1937 and was finally laid away by a saddened Congress without benefit of presidents.

The year Professor Tugwell described this "first step" the Socialist party met in national convention assembled at Milwaukee and adopted a platform and named candidates calling for the "socialization of banking," all natural resources, basic industries and utilities, curbing the United States Supreme Court, employment, health, and accident insurance, $5 billions for immediate federal relief, and another $5 billions for public works, etc.

We come to 1939. We note that although Rexford Guy Tugwell had by then left Washington, Tugwellism had not, nor the gospel according to St. Marx. In 1939, Adolf Berle, Jr., before the Temporary National Economic Committee, said, "The theory that a bank must 'make a profit' today has ceased to be valid, except in an extremely limited sense. . . . In the sense, however, that a bank is 'entitled' to a profit or a reward for something or other (sic) there seems to be *no reason for its existence.*" Of course, to say that a credit institution is entitled to no profit is the same as to say that capital, and the thrifty people who saved it, are entitled to no profit. This is socialism de luxe.

How does this compare with the program overseas? Lenin said, "One state bank as huge as possible, with branches in every factory is *nine-tenths* of the socialist apparatus. . . . Through the nationalization of the banks they '—the small business men—' *may be tied hand and foot.*"

The British Socialist leader, G. D. H. Coles, puts it this way: "Before a labor government nationalizes any industry, it should first nationalize the banks. With the banks in our hands *we can take over other industries at leisure.*"

Yes, Karl Marx has immigrated to the United States. And like some other immigrants he smuggled himself in unaware. His coming was not announced. In fact, whenever his policies have been openly advocated they have been universally turned down by the American people.

For example, in 1936, out of 45,646,817 votes for president, Norman Thomas, socialist candidate, got 187,720 and Earl Browder, communist, got 80,159, total for the two disciples of Marx, 267,879, or 1 vote in 170.

In 1932, out of 39,816,522 votes for president, Thomas, socialist, got 844,781; Reynolds, socialist-labor, 33,276; and Foster, communist, 102,991, total for the three, 981,048, or 1 vote in 40. Between 1932 and 1936 the vote for outright Marxian candidates fell off 713,169, or 72 per cent.

In 1928, out of 36,879,414 votes for president: Thomas, socialist, got 267,420; Foster, communist, 48,770, and Reynolds, socialist-labor, 21,603; total for the three, 337,793, or 1 vote in 109.

These figures appear to warrant "smoke-screen" as descriptive of this creeping collectivism. The American people have never voted for a socialist program. They have repeatedly and overwhelmingly voted it down. Even in our year of greatest distress, 1932, the collectivist vote was less than 3 per cent of the total, one vote in 40. The other 39 voted for the Democratic and Republican platforms of that year—both American.

Yet by indirection, by subterfuge, by boring from within, by the "Trojan horse" technique, we are far down the collectivist trail. Under the "smoke-screen" of an *advertised* better social order, and under the pressure of hard times we have unwittingly embraced "the seeming truth which cunning times put on to entrap the wisest."

But must the program go full circle before we rouse ourselves? Are we to justify the contempt had for us by the "intelligentsia" that it will "be comparatively easy to dynamite the industrial system" as was said by Rexford Guy

Tugwell?   Are we going to wait until not only our economic liberty but our personal, religious and civil liberties as well are destroyed before we take up the gauntlet of the modern Caesars?   And then, will it be too late?

*   *   *   *   *   *   *

"With the bank crash of 1931, the Reich attained a position from which it dominates more than three-fourths of all German banking, and owns about forty per cent of their shares. . . .

"When this life saving expedition was over, the Reich was the dictator of the whole German banking world.

"The German Reich is one of the largest holding companies, through its ownership of the 'Viag' (Vereinigte Industrie Unternehmugen A.G.) which in turn is the holding company of a bank, of iron and machine plants, electric light and power concerns, and of a shipping company.

"The German State Railway, the Reichsbahn, is the largest company of its kind in the world, with an invested capital in 1932 of about twenty-six billion marks and with a personnel of about 720,000.

"The Reich has an aluminum monopoly, and important participations in coal and potash mines.

"Prussia invaded the banking field with the Prussian State Bank and Girozentrale.   She owns the large 'Preussag,' the Prussian Mining and Foundry Company.

"Prussia has gone heavily into farming as a part of the agricultural relief system, and she has bought tens of thousands of acres for colonization."

—From the chapter "The State Goes Into Business" in *The New Deal in Europe,* by Emil Lengyel.

3

SOCIALISM THROUGH THE BACK DOOR

WHEN SPEAKER GARNER on May 31, 1932, appointed the "Shannon" Committee to investigate government competition with private enterprise I was reluctant to serve. It was my first term in Congress; I knew I had a hard campaign for re-election that fall and I felt I could not afford to be away from home attending committee meetings. I have not forgotten what the Speaker told me, "Take it, boy. It will do you more good than kissing every baby in your district." Wise man.

I took it and came back to Congress by the biggest majority a Democrat had ever received in my district.

Despite the lengthening shadows of that depression year the country was ripe for our investigation—the first in that line ever attempted. Hearings were held in Washington, Kansas City, St. Louis, Lawton, my home town of South Bend (following a tip from Cactus Jack), Memphis, New Orleans, New York and Chicago. Six hundred and twenty-five witnesses clamored to be heard. And they were heard—sympathetically. They represented 225 lines of business in which the Federal government was already competing with them. They felt unjustly treated and poured out their stories with an intensity of feeling I have never forgotten.

The investigation was nonpartisan despite the fact that the Republican party, having been in power for 12 years, was more responsible for the conditions complained of than the Jeffersonians.

As a Democrat I took a quiet comfort from the fact that our party platform adopted in June of that year pledged "the removal of Government from all fields of private enterprise except where necessary to develop public works and natural resources in the public interest." With this "covenant with the people to be faithfully kept by the party when entrusted with power" endorsed by our presidential candidate "one hundred per cent," I felt on solid ground, not only as an American, but as a Democrat.

Whatever centralizing tendencies the Republican party may have exhibited I felt that Democrats at least could be trusted not to become socialists, that they would not only refuse further to invade the "fields of private enterprise," but would "remove" government from all such fields it then occupied, with the exceptions noted in the platform. We had entered into a "contract" with the people wherein we "solemnly promised by appropriate action to put into effect the principles, policies and reforms herein advocated, and to eradicate the policies, methods and practices herein condemned."

On this rock I took my stand. It has disturbed me profoundly to have since witnessed the moral disintegration that has swept over the entire world. Treaties to "renounce war as instruments of national policy" are scraps of paper, piracy has returned to the high seas, wars are fought with callous indifference to even declaring them, contracts are cynically rewritten or discarded by the stronger party, the property rights of honest, hard working men are held in contempt, political war is declared against thrift and the principle of thrift—which is the soul of free enterprise, as against the compulsion of the State. And party platforms, "covenants with the people," have been infected with this cancer of moral decay.

I say again, as in the previous chapter, that not only have the American people never voted *for* national socialism; they overwhelmingly and specifically voted *against* it in 1932 by ratifying this "covenant with the people" pledging the removal of government from the fields of private enterprise.

Many of my friends think this moral rot has gone so deep in the body politic that it is beyond healing. If so, the republic is doomed and fascism will soon be our fate, with communism our remoter legacy to posterity. Benjamin Franklin once said that our government "can only end in despotism as other forms have done before it when people have become so *corrupted* as to need despotic government, being incapable of any other."

I have not lost faith that the heart of this great people is still sound. I believe they love their children as our fathers loved us. I know that 64,000,000 of them, over forty per cent more than ever voted for presidential candidates of all parties, in life insurance policies alone, have a *stake* in the survival of private enterprise. I believe that events abroad and at home are causing a worldwide moral revulsion. I believe that a spiritual renaissance is not far off. I believe the day is not yet lost when the American people will rally by the tens of millions around some leader with the unyielding granite of a Grover Cleveland, inflexible in his defense of "this last best hope of earth."

Such is my creed. And I am *happier* fighting for it than I could possibly be in conceding the field as lost—

> "For how can men die better,
> Than facing fearful odds
> For the ashes of their fathers
> And the temples of their gods"?

And you, who read these lines, will it be said of you with deep rebuke, "Hang yourself, brave Crillon, we fought at Arques and you were not there"? I will answer that. I believe you are going to get into the fight.

As Roy W. Moore, president of Canada Dry, recently said, "What will it avail us to sweat blood to build up our business if the majority of Americans should decide that our system of free enterprise has outlived its usefulness, and that the only way out, is to swing over to totalitarianism along the lines established in Russia, Germany, Italy? We must take time off our daily round of duties to convince the people that it was the American Way—which gives the workers and all other classes in this country the best living conditions on the face of the earth."

To return to the Shannon Committee. Although I have mentioned the Democratic platform of 1932, I intend no partisanship in this discussion. The Republican members of that Committee—Hon. Robert F. Rich of Pennsylvania and Hon. William H. Stafford of Wisconsin—were unanimous in joining the Committee report. And here let me say that the real division in America today is not between the Republican and Democratic parties as history has known them. It is between the men and women of *both* parties who would save free institutions and those who would destroy them. The first group is still in a huge majority in this country, but the struggle will require their common action. I am not thinking of any formal coalition. That is probably impossible, nor is it necessary. Those who think alike are not incapable of acting together, as they proved with respect to the Supreme Court bill of 1937.

I will not review at length the findings of the Shannon Committee. But a tear should be shed for its untimely end. We were obliged to file our report in early 1933 and did so on February 8th of that year. Unfortunately it was drowned out from public hearing by the crash of bank doors closing in Detroit, and then, like falling dominoes, throughout the Union.   And so, "Alas, poor Yorick.   I knew him well."

The blanketing out of that report I have always regarded as one of the major casualties of the depression. Under auspicious circumstances I have steadfastly believed its recommendations would have been accepted, and the ground lost to state socialism would have not only been regained, but a new Maginot line might have been erected to defend our free enterprise system against alien philosophies.

The 225 lines of enterprise whose fields government had already invaded in 1932 included:

Agriculture
Amusements
Architecture
Baking
Banking
Livestock
Ship chandlery
Printing and binding
Brickmaking
Canning
Brush and broom manufacture
Canvas products
Cement dealers
Chemicals
Clothing
Coal business
Coffee importation
Contracting
The cotton industry
Creameries
Animal and fowl feeds
Fruit and vegetable shippers

Furs
The grain trade
Ice manufacture
Laundries
Mechanical shop and marine
    work
Shoe factories
The wool industry
Dairy farming
Engraving
Envelopes and stationery
Explosives
The express industry
Fertilizer products
Furniture dealers and manu-
    facturing
Gasoline and oils
Hotels and restaurants
Insurance
Lumber
Saddlery and harness manu-
    facture

These and many other businesses have heard the tread of Caesar in the intervening years.   But as this is to be a short survey of the field as it lies before us in 1940, I shall now select, as of first importance, government competition with private enterprise in the field of banking and credit. As stated in the previous chapter, this is the hub of the socialistic wheel. Control here carries control everywhere. This is the Verdun of the farflung battle line of freedom versus feudalism. If government further penetrates at this salient the lines cannot hold and free enterprise is in rout.

Although intended to save and not destroy private banking and credit institutions, the first big step in government banking took place in Mr. Hoover's administration. I refer to the Reconstruction Finance Corporation act passed January 22, 1932.

For whatever of merit or demerit may attach, I was one of 55 members of the House who voted against that bill and was soundly cussed out for doing so. I ventured to express the view at the time that this experiment in government banking would have incalculable consequence in the spread of state socialism.

That this prophecy has been justified by events I believe few will deny. Nevertheless, I am not wise enough to say where the long balance of good or harm may lie. It was one of those "hard cases which make bad law." It was promoted in good faith to check the avalanche of deflation. It was intended to stop the run on banks, although it failed to do so. And it was intended to serve an emergency condition and then to be discontinued. It had a two-year time limitation. Then it was to stop!

For the historian I record one argument for the 55 who voted "No." In the "Cleveland panic" the government came to the rescue of no one. Liquidation did take place. Creditors took over where debtors left off. It was violent while it lasted, but here is a point to remember. It did not last long. In three years the depression was over and the nation had begun to climb the hill again, freed from the weight of dead horses. Our depression has lasted ten years and the carcasses of nearly fifty billion dead horses clutter the landscape—as witness our government debt. There are also other casualties of convalescence!

Nevertheless, R.F.C. was passed with the blessing of bankers, insurance executives and railroad presidents. Then the process I thought I foresaw developed. "You have taken care of the bankers. Are you going to let the little fellow go to the wall?" And the R.F.C. with a two year life in 1932 has been broadened by amendment not less than thirty times and continued in existence by the very pressures it begot.

As of its February, 1940, statement R.F.C. has authorized loans totaling $13,414,960,851.91 since it was organized. Of this amount actual disbursements now total $10,483,819,997.22, with repayments of $5,833,615,408.24. In addition to repayments Congress wrote off as a loss $2,720,255,177.07, which R.F.C. had disbursed to Mr. Harry Hopkins and other government agencies.

But this does not tell the whole story of Uncle Sam, Banker, Unlimited. The following are some of his branch banks and lending agencies in addition to the Reconstruction Finance Corporation:

Central Bank for Cooperatives
Commodity Credit Corporation
Disaster Loan Corporation
District Banks for Cooperatives
Electric Home and Farm Authority
Emergency Crop and Feed Loan Office
Export-Import Bank of Washington
Farm Credit Administration
Farm Security Administration
Federal Credit Unions
Federal Deposit Insurance Corporation
Federal Emergency Administration of Public Works
Federal Farm Mortgage Corporation
Federal Home Loan Banks
Federal Housing Administration

Federal Intermediate Credit Banks
Federal Land Banks
Federal Reserve Banks
Federal Savings and Loan Associations
Federal Savings and Loan Insurance Corporation
Home Owners' Loan Corporation
Housing Division, Public Works Administration
Indiana Rehabilitation Loan Office
Inland Waterways Corporation
Land Bank Commissioner
National Farm Loan Associations
National Mortgage Associations
Production Credit Associations
Production Credit Corporation
Puerto Rican Reconstruction Administration
Reconstruction Finance Mortgage Company
Regional Agricultural Credit Corporation
Resettlement Administration
Rural Electrification Administration
Tennessee Valley Authority
United States Housing Authority
United States Maritime Commission
United States Postal Savings System

Whether from the bird's-eye view of a balance sheet political banking will prove any more successful than private banking, time alone will tell. At this point the HOLC experience in New York State is interesting to the citizen stockholder, whose chief function may be to meet assessments disguised as taxes. As of February, 1940, in New York State alone, HOLC had 80,415 residence loans, totalling $411,276,352. Of these Uncle Sam has had to take over 25,754, or 32 per cent. The average out of pocket loss on 5,863 homes so far resold has been $2,803 exclusive of selling costs. If this rate is maintained a loss is indicated on the 25,754 repossessed of $72,188,422 in *one* state. It is not possible to estimate future losses but it is apparent that the thrifty home owners of the nation who have struggled to pay their own debts will have to dig deeper to pay other people's debts. This is called in the trade the "socialization of debt." The fortunate liquidate the unfortunate. The workers support the shirkers. The bees feed the drones.

Let this government banking proceed step by step and every home mortgagor, every farm borrower, and every business will in fact be "bound hand and foot." Destroy private banks, take over insurance, give government an "exclusive monopoly" of credit, as Herr Marx recommends, and then indeed "business will logically be required to disappear" and "with the banks in our hands we can take over other industries at leisure." Their leisure, not ours!

4

TAXATION SUCKS THE EGGS

Extrah! all about it. United States Steel declares dividend of $5.61 a share to the government, or a total of $48,842,131.

Extrah! Special! Steel declares dividend to its owners of nothing a share, or a total of nothing. Get a paper, mister.

That is not the way the newsboys called it. But it is the way it happened in 1938. Government got a nest egg; the owners got a goose egg. The 168,399 common stockholders who owned United States Steel got nothing from a year's operations. The government—federal, state and local—got almost 49 millions. The investors had contributed their money to support the bureaucrats. The pay rollers got it in the pockets; the owners got it in the neck.

These figures support the main thesis of this book—that we are marching toward a species of National Socialism in which the paper titles to property will be left in their "owners," but the management and earnings will be taken over by government. This is the way Hitler makes the Germans goosestep. It is not government ownership. It is not communism. No confiscation of property! Property is still respected. You keep your hens. Give us the eggs!

It will be said that one swallow does not make a summer. Granted. So let us add 149 other swallows to United States Steel.

The American Federation of Investors has compiled the taxes and common stock dividends for 150 companies. The list includes only one company with assets of more than $5 billion. It includes United States Steel; A.T. & T.; Armour; B. & O. R.R.; Caterpillar Tractor; Chrysler; Continental Oil; DuPont; Eastman Kodak; Illinois Central R.R.; National Cash Register; Montgomery Ward; New York Central Railroad; Ohio Oil; Quaker Oats; R.C.A.; Socony-Vacuum; Standard of Indiana; Swift; Texas Corporation; Westinghouse and others.

That the 150 companies were representative of American enterprise is shown by the fact that they had total assets of $42 billions. The year was 1937, the best under the New Deal. In that year the average dividends for each share of common stock was $1.95, and the average total tax—federal, state and local—per share was $2.62 or 34 per cent *more to government than to the owners.* Government, which made no direct investment in a $42 billion plant got more out of its operations than the investors.

Another way of putting it based on the average per company, is that before each common stockholder got anything, government got $291. For each employe government got $514. This means that government held a first lien upon each stockholder's investment of $291 for that year. It means, too, that if there were no taxes, these 150 companies *might have paid each of their workers $514 more a year in wages,* or $42.83 a month. Or, the companies might have sold their product for that much less, thus increasing their sales, which in turn would have increased production and put "Men Wanted" signs over the gate.

Total taxes paid by 124 of these companies in 1932 were $681,648,286. In 1937 it was $1,631,284,094, or nearly one billion dollars more. That extra billion, if government had not taken it, might have employed one million men at $1,000 a year!

Taxation sucks the eggs. Money paid for taxes cannot be paid for wages, nor for raw materials, nor for dividends.

In 1938, 7,806 industrial corporations did business in Wisconsin. From current operations, after paying for materials, freight, wages, etc., these companies made $91,-551,830. But their total taxes were $112,158,743. In other words, after paying taxes the total industry of Wisconsin made *nothing whatever* from operations.

Taxation sucked Wisconsin eggs to the tune of $91 millions, and $20,606,913 in addition.

On April 29, 1938, President Roosevelt sent a message to Congress from which sprang the Temporary National Economic Committee. What Mr. Roosevelt said in that message was, to me, wholly admirable. It is one of the soundest papers he has ever produced. Among other things, he wrote, "The individual must be encouraged . . . to venture his own small savings, not in stock gambling, but in new enterprise investment."

Later, on May 16, 1939, Mr. Roosevelt wrote to Senator O'Mahoney, Chairman of TNEC, a letter in which he said, "It is a matter of common knowledge that the dollars which the American people save each year are not yet finding their way back into productive enterprise in sufficient volume to keep our economic machine turning over at the rate required to bring about full employment. . . . It is our task to bring together the men, machines and money."

We know that "new enterprise investment" is not being made except in a trickle when it should be a mighty river bearing the commerce and the hope of a nation.

Witness these Federal Reserve Board figures of new corporate capital issues:

	millions
1923	$2,635
1924	3,029
1925	3,605
1926	3,754
1927	4,657
1928	5,346
1929	8,002
1930	4,483
1931	1,551
1932	325
1933	161
1934	178
1935	404
1936	1,192
1937	1,227
1938	854

For the six years, 1933–1938 inclusive, new capital investment totaled less than it did for the single year 1930. It averaged $669 millions a year. For the ten years, 1923–1932 it averaged $3,739 millions a year.

For comparison it would be more fair to exclude the mushroom period of 1927–1928–1929. Let us take only the years 1923–1924–1925. In many government indices these three years are taken as par = 100. They followed the crash of 1921 and preceded the big boom of 1929 by four to six years. If we have had a normal period since the World War this was it. New capital investment for this par period averaged $3,090 millions.

Contrast $3,090 with the 1933–1938 average of $669. The latter is only 22 per cent of the former. In "shooting for par," we have fallen short by 78 per cent and this, too, takes no account of the increase of population in the 10 to 15 years that have intervened.

Why is "new enterprise investment" not being made? Certainly one of the correct answers is that taxation sucks the eggs.

We have given two bird's-eye views of American industry—150 "Big Business" companies operating all over the country, and 7,806 companies, most of them "little business," operating in Wisconsin.

Consider the prospective investor in any of these companies, big or little, or in any new company which might be organized. He is thinking of buying common stock. He knows preferred stock and notes or bonds will have to come ahead of him. But he knows, also, that government —federal, state and local—holds a prior mortgage ahead of everybody, and on every dollar that may be made. He knows that this government mortgage and its annual accruals must be paid, in large part, even if the company makes nothing. He knows that the total taken by government in 1938 was 22.4% of total national income.

Government, first preferred stockholder in all American business, had prior dividends *guaranteed* of 22.4%. And a deferred, but preferred, claim of 5.6% (government borrowing), or a total of $28 out of $100 of earnings!

But that is not everything our investor has to think of. If 28% were *all* the "take" of government he might "venture his own small savings" in something that looked real rosy. But he doesn't know that is *all*. He knows government costs are constantly going up. For example, Westinghouse Electric in 1934 paid taxes of $2,500,000; in 1935, $5,000,000; in 1936 $9,000,000; in 1937 $16,000,000!

And more to come. Social "security" taxes alone are due to go up to nine cents on every dollar of wages.

Our investor, therefore, is asked to put his money into a business in which there is a first preferred stockholder (the government) who has the power to declare an increase of *his* dividends *at any time!* This is like asking him to buy a farm plastered with a 5 per cent mortgage which the mortgage holder may at any time increase to 10 or 15 or 22.4 or 28 per cent interest!

And still some people profess to wonder why, instead of

the old surging, dynamic America we have a country that
is groggy, punch drunk.

These dollars that the investor would *like* to venture in
a dynamic, expanding America are being put in government bonds or lie idle in the banks. They do not go into
business largely because of the heavy and uncertain tax.
They go into the "cyclone cellar" of government bonds
largely because they are *not* taxed.

The result is that by a creeping paralysis we are na-
tionalizing the savings of the nation and investing them
in debt. This debt is not re-creative, self-liquidating. It
is not like wool on a sheep's back. Our collateral is a dead
horse.

We should remove the tax exempt feature on all government bonds, particularly federal bonds. We should make
it hard—and expensive—for government to borrow
money! That would put brakes on the socialist chariot.

Well, people say, "You can't let them starve." Right.
No one is going to starve. But this starving fetish as an
alibi for constructive thinking is badly overworked. The
fact is that only one tax dollar in six goes to keep people
from starving. You can keep people from starving and
still reduce taxes and unless we reduce taxes we will never
see the old Pikes-Peak-or-Bust United States again.

The fact is that "our workers may never see a tax bill
but they pay in *deduction from wages,* in increased cost
of what they buy, or in *broad cessation of employment.*"

Sir William Flinders Petrie, archeologist, who knows
more than any man living about civilizations that have
died and men who have starved, says that democracies
eat themselves through excessive taxation until they col-
lapse and are succeeded by the Man on Horseback or the
rank growth of the jungle.

Few things would do more to insure Americans from

ever starving than a national determination that taxes
shall not go up, and will come down.

We read in the Good Book that "it came to pass in
those days, that there went out a decree from Caesar
Augustus that *all the world* should be taxed."

History repeats itself. Cities, states and the nation are
in a feverish scramble to tax all the world. Like West
Indians, they are now diving for pennies. New commodities and occupations are being taxed, rates are going up, exemptions are going down.

For example, note the increase of the federal surtax on
income:

Year	Exemption	Rate
1926............	$10,000	From 1 to 20 per cent
1932............	6,000	" 1 to 55 " "
1934............	4,000	" 4 to 59 " "
1936............	4,000	" 4 to 75 " "

The growth of the federal tax on estates is as follows:

Year	Exemption	Rate
1926............	$100,000	From 1 to 20 per cent
1932............	50,000	" 1 to 45 " "
1934............	50,000	" 1 to 60 " "
1935............	10,000	" 2 to 70 " "

On the highest income bracket Uncle Sam now takes
79 per cent and on the highest estate bracket 70 per cent.
Meantime, and in addition, the states are taxing income
and inheritance at a constantly increasing rate and cities
are beginning to tax incomes—three taxes on the same income. Proceeds of life insurance, or annuities, formerly
wholly free from inheritance tax, are finding the amount
exempt decreasing and the rate increasing. Security for
old age for the thrifty American is melting away. In
addition recent decisions of the United States Supreme
Court are subjecting intangibles to double or triple taxa-

tion, even if, as a result, an inheritance is completely wiped out, leaving nothing for the heirs. Socialism marches on!

I said security for old age is melting away. The pension fund of the Protestant Episcopal Church in 1933 was $29,447,000. It yielded an income for aged ministers and their widows of $1,447,851. In 1938 the principal, through gifts, had increased to $34,192,000, but the yield had decreased to $945,923. In short, $4,745,000 more of principal yielded $501,928 less of income. How secure do these aged ministers feel? And this same process, in one way or another, is undermining every pension fund in America, school teachers, police, firemen, railroad and industrial employes, all savings bank depositors, some 35,-000,000, and all holders of life insurance. It is time for them to wake up!

One of the largest life insurance companies announced, effective December 15, 1939, that due "to the increasing number of states taxing annuity premiums and the prevailing low interest rates" it was necessary for that company to make the third increase in five years of the price of life annuities. An annuity now costs, in that company, 17.5 per cent more for the same protection.

The per capita public debt in 1938, as computed by the National Industrial Conference Board was $432.65. This was greater than the per capita public debt in Germany, Italy or France! In two of these countries a desperate people have turned to National Socialism. Drowning men grasp at straws.

No member of Congress has done a more useful job than my friend Albert J. Engel of Michigan. State by state, county by county, he has translated this debt into terms of a mortgage upon the entire property—real estate, lands, buildings and personal property—of the whole country. According to Representative Engel the national debt alone (exclusive of state and municipal debt) on June 30 of this year (1940) will equal 34 per cent of the assessed value of every piece of real and personal property in the 48 states. In some states the total public debt—federal, state and municipal—is more than the total assessed value. In Arkansas, Florida and South Carolina, the debt is up to 190 per cent of the assessed value of all property. In the wealthier states it is: Illinois, 68%; Ohio, 33%; Pennsylvania, 34%; New York, 30%. In these calculations the state's share of the *federal* debt is based on per cent of total population living in the state.

It must be something of a shock to the farmer in the Illinois corn belt to realize that his farm has an invisible and unrecorded first mortgage against it of 68 per cent of its assessed value. It is only government (and politicians) who can incur debt and make someone else pay for it.

Don't tell the farmer that the rich will pay the bill. He knows better. Taxes on farm lands and buildings are 155 per cent greater than before the war—not the present war—but the one in which we tried to straighten out the universe. If he paid $100 then, he pays $255 now. This tax burden depresses all real estate values. Any prospective buyer has to figure the tax as a first charge against earnings and it is interesting to note that the Department of Commerce in June, 1939, announced that the assessed value of American property subject to taxes had declined $24,311,000,000 from 1932 to 1937. As values declined $24 billion, the federal debt increased $17 billion. More debt against less value. This is working both sides of the street or, to change the simile, it is putting the thrifty American between the upper and nether millstones. In 1938, according to a treasury report, the total tax burden —federal, state and local—was 79.6 per cent greater than in 1932.   The taxes paid by many petroleum companies exceed their total wage payments to workers.

Meantime, as National Socialism marches on, we have legislation on the calendar of Congress to impose another billion a year for state medicine and a fifth of a billion a year for federal education.   The worker bees are to be further taxed to support the drones.   Those who go without to pay their doctor are to be taxed to pay the bills of those who spend six times their average annual doctor's bill for liquor, candy, cosmetics, amusements and gambling.

In summary, it may be said: That excessive taxation and the uncertainty of further increases, is making it difficult for free enterprise to expand, or even continue; that it discourages wealth creation and destroys jobs; that government deficit financing, under which the government borrows as cheaply as possible, with consequent low interest rates for savings, is undermining the security of the hardworking American, the kind who made the nation and every community in it; that it works to the advantage of the large and established business and to the disadvantage of the new or small business, without reserves; that it is burning the powder of national defense, exhausting our credit for future emergencies.

But more fundamental, this political war against the *savings* of thrift, is eroding the *principle* of thrift and the character and courage of thrifty men and women.   In doing that it strikes at the foundation of the American system of government and free enterprise.

It does it in this way: With the exception of the artist, poet, patriot or scientist, who labors for the joy of satisfying an inner hunger, there are, and have always been just two incentives for the creation of wealth, the hope of reward or the lash of the slave.

The hope of reward is the spark plug of free enterprise. It is the principle of thrift. It is the desire of man to be a man, self-supporting and self-respecting, and not the galley slave or pensioner of the State. That incentive and the freedom America has given it has released millions of springs of human energy and ambition. In doing this it has brought more new wealth into the world than all previous feudalisms, added together.

Because the Constitution of the United States is wrapped around this principle of reward for individual effort our form of government is the negation of National Socialism. The Federal Government was given only specific powers, mostly to regulate and police. It was never intended by our fathers for the Federal Government to undertake business enterprise as such. That power was one of the great powers "reserved to the people."

An attack, therefore, upon the savings of honest thrift and the *principle of thrift,* is an attack upon the American form of government itself. This, Democrats and Republicans alike, must resist.

    *   *   *   *   *   *   *

Chickens are coming home to roost. When men like Senators Byrd, Bailey, Glass, Vandenburg, Taft and Harrison, and Congressmen Rich, Ludlow, Woodrum, Taber and others began to ask "Where will you get the money?" it was considered a big laugh. But it is no longer a joke. A study recently made by the National Association of Credit Men shows that the repercussion of rapidly rising taxes on credit and employment is becoming serious. It is particularly serious to the "little business man." If continued, business will continue to flow to the industrial giants which are able to survive by reason of huge resources and administered prices for their products.

This study covered 430 companies, all small or medium sized, located in 40 states and having a total invested capital of $650,000,000. I quote as follows:

"Any company which is paying out a steadily increasing part of its profits for federal, state and local taxes, must either find some means of increasing its income or be forced to present a less satisfactory report of its financial condition when requesting an extension of credit. That is particularly true in the case of smaller companies with comparatively limited financial resources. The companies may have a good reputation and good prospects but their diminishing profit ratio, after payment of taxes, will, nevertheless, impair their ability to obtain the amount of credit which may be essential to their continued or expanded operations or even to their very existence.

"In fact, it is not unlikely that this development has materially contributed to the demand for direct governmental financial aid to small business. It may be remarked in that connection, however, that companies whose growing tax load makes them less desirable credit risks to private credit grantors *are no better risks to the government*."

Chiefly on account of "Social Security" taxes, one small manufacturer in 1935 made $33,000 in profits before taxes of which it paid a total of 27 per cent. In 1938 it made $10,800 of which it paid 52 per cent to Uncle Sam and 46 per cent to state and city, 98 per cent in all. Out of the remaining 2 per cent the owners are expected to pay nothing to themselves, but to hire more men! Many paid out in taxes in 1938 more than they made.

Several instances were reported "where payrolls had already been reduced for the purpose of relieving the social security tax burden." Mr. Roosevelt once predicted a "broad cessation of employment," as a result of excessive taxation.

For a parallel we turn to *A History of National Socialism*, by Konrad Heiden (Alfred A. Knopf, publisher). The author writes:

"The deduction is obvious; there was increased activity in business, but it was less lucrative. Production and turnover increased, but the total income, the spending power of the people, diminished. . . . Whether prices rise in Germany and thus decrease the participation of the consumer in the social product; or whether the prices are kept forcibly down and thus wages are lowered, in any case Germany . . . is striving toward a form of life which Schacht has described with some frankness as 'industrial self denial and a readiness to do with a smaller amount of luxuries.' "

5

THE BLIGHT OF BUREAUCRACY

DURING THE fight against the packing of the United States Supreme Court I had several letters from Newton D. Baker, former Secretary of War. I recall vividly he wrote in one of them that if the Supreme Court in its long career had done no more than to protect us (until then) from administrative absolutism it would have well earned the gratitude of the nation. He referred to the constant effort of bureaucracy to be lawmaker, complainant, detective, prosecutor, witness, judge, jury, and executioner.

But the bureaucratic tide is now not only sweeping aside the rights of the citizen, as witness NLRB. It is an evil thing for other reasons: 1, Its costs; 2, its throttling effect upon business; 3, its damage to free elections, through its rapidly growing pay roll vote; 4, its control over Congress whereby constitutional and representative government is rapidly, although subtly, being transformed into an administrative legislature, not elected by nor responsible to a free people.

My former colleagues—Hon. James M. Beck, in "Our Wonderland of Bureaucracy," and Hon. Louis L. Ludlow, in "America Go Bust"—writing from their vantage point on Capitol Hill, have described this centipede as it was some years ago. It would be a monumental task to even catalog its million feet today.

Yes, million. Compared with 563,000 in January, 1933, there are now 933,000 persons in the *executive* branch of the *federal* government alone. This excludes Congress and its employes, all federal judges, marshals, and clerks; everyone connected with the army and navy; all persons on relief; all farmers drawing subsidy checks; all contractors working for Uncle Sam; and, of course, it excludes all employes of the 175,000 state, county, city, town and township governments which have the sovereign power to levy taxes. All told, and for all governments, for 1937–38, there were 3,788,616 persons employed by government and paid with tax money, not counting WPA workers and farm subsidees. As the Treasury reported in January, 1940, the total pay roll to these nearly four million employes alone is $5,506,874,000. At three dependents to the worker we have here some 15,000,000 who are paid by the taxpayer. If all farmers in the nation gave up 70 per cent of all their crops to them this would be the equivalent in dollar cost of government pay-rollers.

But we speak of federal executive bureaucrats only, 933,000 in number. This is 14,894 above the previous high watermark on November 11, 1918. In the gain of 370,000 since Mr. Roosevelt was inaugurated (on an economy platform) there are about 100,000 employed by agencies not previously in existence, for example, TVA, with 14,313 on its pay roll.

This may be a good point to state that with a few exceptions, the fact that 933,000 persons are in the administrative or executive branch is the immediate responsibility of the President of the United States. It is not alone that he and his predecessors may have urged the creation of these bureaus, nor that in his budget messages he urged the appropriations for their hire.

The fact is that after Congress has authorized the creation of a bureau, and voted appropriations for its support, the Executive is not required by any law whatever to hire any particular number of employes. Congress may have been at fault in its function. Nevertheless, that is no alibi to the Executive. He can reduce personnel and expenses any time he chooses.

He is not obliged to spend all the money appropriated. At this moment the Executive could save scores of millions of dollars by a simple order to the heads of his departments and bureaus.

This was made perfectly clear in May, 1932, by Congressman Beck, former Solicitor General, and probably the ranking lawyer in the 72nd Congress. He said, "If the President would tell each member of his Cabinet to appoint three discreet men to go through each department and ascertain the employes that did not do an honest day's work, it would develop at once why this is the most over-manned government in the world."

This was in 1932, a Republican Congressman criticizing a Republican president. Mr. Beck pointed out that ever since 1926, when the Supreme Court decided Myers v. United States, 272 U.S. 52, Congress cannot, even if it would, impose any restrictions whatever on the Executive power of removal, even of officers whose appointment, in the first instance, required the "advice and consent of the Senate."

So there is a plain remedy for reducing the fungus growth. Congress could do it by refusing to vote the money. But even if Congress votes the money the president is not obliged to spend it. (With a few exceptions.) The president can slash expenses any time he wants to.

For the fiscal year 1941, President Roosevelt estimates the dollar cost of merely administering the regular government departments will be $952,239,610. This is exclusive of the cost of relief, aids to agriculture, aids to youth, national defense, interest on the debt, public works, social security, veterans, and the expense of administering the same.

But the dollar cost, nearly one billion dollars, is only part of the bill to the taxpayers. For example, the Central Statistical Board has reported that in a single year 135,-700,000 federal forms, questionnaires and returns were filed. 21,000,000 of these were filed by farmers, averaging 3 per farm per year, and 60,000,000 by industry, finance, commerce, trade, averaging 20 a year by each person or company required to file.

This, of course, does not include returns made to 48 states, 3,000 counties, etc. One company, and by no means the largest, filed 34,000 *tax* returns alone in a single year, averaging more than 100 per working day.

The 60,000,000 forms filed by industry, etc., asked an average of 65 questions each, or nearly 4 billion questions in all. Small retail stores filed 10 returns a year, averaging 50 questions. Automobile companies filed 250 returns a year, and railroad companies 1,000 annually, or 3 per working day. The figures in this paragraph refer only to the *federal* government. They help to explain why the "tired business man" gets that way.

In Germany, on an international barter trade of 10,000 pounds of wool for toys, 680 forms had to be filled in. The Nazi bureaucracy issues 700 to 1,000 special ordinances every week to control or regulate German business. (Economic Development of Germany under National Socialism—1937—National Industrial Conference Board.) The total number of ordinances, rules, regulations, administrative decisions, statutes, federal, state and local, regulating our business in the United States cannot be known. But the total may not be much less, and may far exceed the Nazi bureaucracy. They pose one possible answer to the question why American business has lost its forward stride.

If this be thought to be "reactionary" I cite the view

of one of the great liberals, Justice Benjamin Cardozo, discussing a Federal Statute (Standard Chemical and Metals Corp. v. Waugh Chem. Corp., 131 N.E. 566). He said that when we put by government by law for government by men "the individual is set adrift upon the uncharted sea of subjective prejudice and favor."

The bureaucratic decision he says, "unrestrained and unrestricted, becomes the test of right and wrong, and men are viewed as malefactors for failure to consent *to the unknown and unknowable.*" Business planning becomes a fortune telling affair, with hired soothsayers and political prophets examining the entrails of bureaucracy to guess whether the citizen may venture forth to the market place.

The Sherman Anti-Trust Act is an illustration. Although that has been on the statute books for 50 years, the United States Government remains without a settled policy with respect to its interpretation. Every incoming attorney-general creates new uncertainties to the managers of American business. What will his policy be? Will it be a strict enforcement or what might be termed a "common sense" enforcement? Will the incoming administration follow the policies of its predecessor? Will it favor reasonable efforts not involving monopoly or contracts in restraint of trade which may tend to stabilize the conditions under which an industry must operate and, hence, stabilize employment?

Does the new administration want prices generally to rise or to fall? In the early years of Mr. Roosevelt's administration, it appeared to be his policy, by legislative and administrative action, to restore prices to the 1926 level. Suddenly, in the spring of 1937 and long before the 1926 level of commodity prices had been reached, the President announced that copper and other basic materials were too high. In the field of agricultural commodities there has been a constant effort to lift them to prices prevailing before the World War of 1914 or at least to so-called "parity" levels.

Another illustration of the unpredictability of policy under which business has labored is NRA. The National Industrial Recovery Act suspended the Sherman Anti-Trust statutes with reference to NRA codes which met presidential approval. It did not suspend the Sherman Act with reference to business understandings not approved by the President. Under NRA, for example, government policy was to support at a minimum level the price of crude petroleum and, hence, of gasoline and other derivatives. After NRA was held unconstitutional by the United States Supreme Court in May, 1935, all efforts to stabilize prices theretofore legal and praiseworthy became overnight, in the eyes of the government, illegal and blameworthy.

A like uncertainty exists with reference to the policies of the Federal Trade Commission. That Commission, in my judgment, is worthy of a greater degree of confidence on the part of business men than they ordinarily attribute to it. It is trying to maintain competition and Fair Trade practices, without which the free enterprise system cannot function. Nevertheless, it is exceedingly difficult for business managers to predict commission policy.

Part of this is one of the inevitable frictions which we must suffer as part of the price for maintaining a democratic form of government. With changing personnel and changing administrations, some uncertainty as to policy is impossible to avoid. Despite this, Congress could make a real contribution toward permanent recovery if it were to review the Sherman Act, Clayton Act, Federal Trade Commission Act and attempt to lay down rules which would eliminate to a far greater extent than now prevails the personal element in interpretation and administration. In

other words, a government of law and not a government of
men. Congress, to the great injury of American business
and their own constituents have too much delegated
to bureaus the determination of policy as well as the
writing of rules and regulations which have the force of
law.

What this bureaucracy costs cannot be measured by
government payrolls and taxes alone. The invisible tax is
enormous. The cost in the value of the time of executives,
the hire of clerks, typists, accountants, engineers, ap-
praisers, lawyers, as well as office rent and adding machines to fill out these 135,700,000 federal forms annually
is staggering. For example, railroads must make returns
to 11 different federal agencies, water carriers to 14, food
manufacturers to 19, retail merchants to 17, banks to 17,
etc. (Report of Central Statistical Board, January, 1939.)
A federal government so disorganized and sprawling as to
require banks to report to 17 different bureaus undertakes
to tell American business how to operate.

But Uncle Sam has much to do and cannot perhaps be
expected to do it well! All this has been foreseen. In
his *Quadregesimo Anno,* Pope Pius XI said, "The State
which was now encumbered with all the burdens once
borne by associations *rendered extinct by it,* was in consequence itself submerged and overwhelmed by an *in-
finity of affairs."*

Dr. Schacht, one time Minister of Economics, said of
German National Socialism, "The new plan is a terrible
thing because it necessarily presupposes an increase in
bureaucracy."

But the Germans went in with their eyes open. They
were up against the gun. It looked like the only way out,
"terrible" as it was. In bitter need of raw materials, imports, rubber, cotton, petroleum, fats, wool, hides, iron,
copper, etc., no gold to pay with: "We must export or die"

in order to pay for imports; quotas and tariffs of their international trade competitors making their export difficult. The difficulty increased by devaluation by England, France and United States of their currencies; under these and other conditions Germany resorted to international barter. This meant, in turn, that government assumed a monopoly of imports, the allocation of raw materials to her industries, the control of exports, and under the necessity to keep export commodities low in price, she assumed an iron control over wages, hours of work, prices, profits, and credit. Under the circumstances National Socialism seemed more logical than starvation.

But they knew what they were doing. There was no smoke-screen, no subterfuge, indirection, sly schemes, no silent reaching for power. It was done openly. They chose tyranny in place of anarchy.

We follow in their footsteps. But by paying lip service to private property and the profit motive the forward movement is screened both as to direction and extent.

*   *   *   *   *   *   *

The Code of Federal Regulations about to be issued by the Government Printing Office will be in 17 volumes, averaging 1,100 pages, or a total of 19,000 pages. This covers only to June 1, 1938, and is exclusive, of course, of the United States Statutes at Large. It is the law written by downtown Washington *after* Congress goes home.

The Government Printing Office in announcing this new publication states that from March 14, 1936 to October 7, 1939, only three and a half years, 115 agencies of the Federal Government issued 14,889 rules, regulations and administrative decisions telling American business how to operate.

The reason God made man last was because He did not want him meddling around while the work was going on!

6

THE NEW DESPOTISM

THE CALLOUS disregard of fundamental decencies by our bureaucrats is gradually coming to light.

We learn that in August, 1939, NLRB entered into an arrangement with the Reconstruction Finance Corporation. Under it NLRB was to notify RFC of any American business against which a "charge" had been made, or was about to be made (sic) that it had been guilty of an unfair labor practice. If the concern had arranged for a loan from the RFC, the latter was to withhold all disbursements to the borrower. We are told that Secretary Perkins' Wage and Hour Division made similar arrangements with the RFC, and that an effort was made to induce the Treasury to do the same with reference to public building construction.

Two points should be stressed. It has never been the rule that a penalty could be imposed upon an American citizen *before* he was found guilty of an offense. In the horse and buggy days, a citizen had first to be found guilty before suffering a penalty. He was entitled to a fair trial before judgment, and judgment before jail.

That is old stuff today. The New Deal in justice is to shut off credit the instant anyone is "charged" with violating the law, or even when he is "about to be charged." The assumption now is that the citizen is guilty first and innocent only if he can prove it.

But this assumes that Congress had in fact authorized the withholding of credit in addition to a fine after the offender, upon due trial, has been found guilty. The case goes deeper. Congress has *not* authorized anyone to withhold credit as an additional punishment for an unfair labor practice, either before or after trial and conviction. NLRB and RFC have therefore secretly undertaken to impose penalties upon American citizens over and above those prescribed by Congress. This is the essence of tyranny. It is government by executive decree. It is not only contemptible; it is cowardly because it was done secretly. The fact that it exists has been disclosed only by reason of the courage and faithfulness of Congressman Howard W. Smith's House Committee, whose creation was opposed as long as possible by the administration.

Let us restate the question: Here is the Jones Company which employs labor. Its business comes within the new definition of interstate commerce and is therefore under the jurisdiction of NLRB. In addition it needs money to expand its operations and employ more men. Congress has authorized it to apply to RFC for a loan. The application is made, the loan granted, and the amount is to be disbursed to the Jones Company from time to time. Relying upon the granting of its loan, the Jones Company extends its operations and makes commitments for raw materials and other expenditures.

At that moment someone whispers to NLRB that the Jones Company has violated the Wagner act. There is no proof that it has done so. There has been no hearing, no trial and perhaps not even a complaint has been filed by any responsible person. In this situation NLRB sends notice to RFC. RFC then cuts off Jones Company's credit.

It can readily be seen that in many, if not most cases, the cutting off of credit is a much more severe penalty than the fine prescribed by Congress, if, in fact, a violation has taken place. It threatens the company with financial ruin. Faced with ruin by this species of bureaucratic despotism, the Jones Company may confess that it is guilty, however innocent it may be.

This is "The New Despotism" as described by Lord Chief Justice Hewart of England in his book by that title. Can it be harnessed in this country before it is too late? A bill is now pending in Congress—the Logan-Walter bill—which is designed to erect some dykes around the vanishing island of liberty. The bill is sponsored by the American Bar Association and many other civic groups. As described by the Senate Judiciary Committee it provides "means and methods whereby the governors may be governed and the regulators regulated." It ought to become law. However it is bitterly opposed by the so-called "liberals." That word "liberal," by the way, is the name of the Trojan Horse! Those who tear down free enterprise and the checks and balances against concentrated power call themselves "liberals."

And so *while he sleeps* the giant Gulliver of American free enterprise is being bound hand and foot by the Lilliputians of government, who singly and recognized, could be brushed aside like flies. Only recently Mr. Roosevelt, by executive order, and over the protests of five great farm organizations, transferred the Farm Credit Administration and its billions of credit facilities, to the Secretary of Agriculture. This removed the FCA from its status as an independent cooperative credit agency, in large part owned and operated by farmers, to what many think will now be a political weapon for control and votes. If NLRB is a sample, the fears are amply justified.

The gradual enslavement of our enterprise to the Wall Street of Washington will proceed along Nazi lines, although we are not supposed to know it. "During the past four years private banks have declined in importance as a source of credit." (Economic Development of Germany Under National Socialism.) Have they not equally in the United States? Insurance companies and banks are finding it difficult to make loans in competition with government lending. Of the latter, Secretary Morgenthau reported to the Senate in February, 1940, in response to Senator Byrd's resolution, that 31 government agencies have loaned nearly $25,000,000,000, and that more than $800,000,000 of real estate has been taken over. The Baltimore *Sun* says that federal agencies "own in part and control in part" more than 2,000 corporations having assets of $4,000,000,000, and have a degree of control, through regulation, loans, subsidies and the fear of "getting in wrong" of more than 23,000 corporations with assets of $70,000,000,000!

But so silently has this Nazification of America gone on that there are many good and patriotic people who think "you are seeing things under the bed" if you tell them we are on the German road. Is life insurance to be next?

One of the most stealthy means by which our bureaucracy marches on is by radio propaganda, as in Germany. In a hearing before a House Committee on a bill written in the Department of the Interior to give Secretary Ickes control of petroleum production, Mr. Russell Brown of the Independent Petroleum Association of America gave some startling testimony which could be read with profit by every American. Mr. Brown testified that under date of February 15, 1939, the National Resources Committee, Frederic Delano, chairman, reported that "Whenever the general public becomes sufficiently *impressed* with the threatened shortage of petroleum products and the possible rise in prices for motor fuel, then the complex problem of regulating the oil and gas industry is likely to be transferred to the federal government."

The way the public was to be *impressed* becomes clear from the script of various radio broadcasts written by the "chief script writer, radio section" of the Interior Department.

As a sample, in one of the scripts it is plain that the whole intent was to promote fear over the loss of petroleum resources, and in so doing discredit the industry itself. The direction for the music is "up wildly and fade" while the sound direction reads, "suggest utter confusion and hysteria of population."

Then come in the following utterances one after the other:

"Doctor: I'm a doctor. I must get there *at once*. A woman is dying!

"Attendant: Sorry, Doc. We haven't a drop of gasoline in the station.

"Sound: Fire Siren.

"Firemen: (Shouting): It's the school house! And we can't move our fire engines!

"Truckdriver: (Through Filter): Listen, boss, I'm carryin' perishable goods—fruit and vegetables—on this truck. How am I gonna get them there before they spoil?

"Ticket Agent: The Twentieth Century Limited can't leave this station, Madam. You'll have to get to New York by stage coach.

"Farmer: (Surprised): Well I'll be doggone. *I can't use my tractor. I can't plow my farm!*

"Husband: (Ordering wife): Get the children. We'll leave the house and find a restaurant where they cook with a *coal* stove!

"Dispatcher: (Droning, via radio): All airplanes are grounded. All airplanes are grounded.

"Boss: You men needn't report to work tomorrow. This plant's shutting down. Can't run our machines without oil.

"Sound: *Telegraph key. In and under.*

"Telegrapher: SOS. SOS. Steamer *America* calling. Stopped in mid ocean. One thousand aboard. Send help at once.

"Admiral: (Dictating): To the Navy Department . . .

Fleet unable to leave port for Pacific coast as ordered. (Fade) Guns useless without oil. Awaiting further word on . . ."

In another broadcast the god-like Narrator says, "I'm speaking for the Department of the Interior. . . . It wouldn't let me say anything that wasn't so." (Imagine!) "You've a Congress that represents you . . . What have you got a Congress for?"

That these broadcasts are dishonest is obvious. The melodramatic effects were all designed to scare people, ignorant that the known petroleum reserves are now greater than at any time in our history. European countries know this technique but it is a new thing in America.

Not only was this an effort to dominate the determination of public policy, and to set up a bureaucratic legislature in defiance of the Constitution which provides that "all legislative powers herein granted shall be vested in a Congress of the United States" (and nowhere else) but it is also an apparent violation of criminal law enacted by Congress to protect itself and the people against such pressure. I refer to United States Code, Title 18, Section 201 enacted July 11, 1919.

This Act of Congress provides that "no part of the money appropriated by any act shall, in the absence of express authorization by Congress, be used, *directly or indirectly* to pay for personal service, advertisement, telegram, telephone, letter, printed or written matter, or *other device,* intended or designed to influence in any manner a member of Congress, to favor or oppose, by vote or otherwise, any legislation or appropriation" with fine and jail penalties for violation.

This act has been cited repeatedly in recent years on the floor of Congress, and as there has been no "express authorization" to my knowledge by which bureaucrats in the government departments may engage in radio broadcasts to propagandize Congress, it seems clear that if the Department of Justice would act, we might reduce the federal payrolls by sending certain officials and their underlings to jail. But I do not indulge in that as a hope. It is merely a thought.

However, as I write, I am glad to report that the House of Representatives has taken cognizance of this effort by government departments to high-pressure Congress. On an amendment offered by Representative Gossett of Texas, the House amended the Interior Department Appropriation Bill by prohibiting that department from using public money "for the broadcast of radio programs designed or calculated to influence the passage or defeat of any legislation pending before Congress."

If the Senate agrees with the House, it will be a good start toward returning to the Congress of the United States its Constitutional independence and integrity as our policy-making body.

The subtle control of radio broadcasters is known to all familiar with federal operations. Licenses are granted for only a few months at a time, they may be suspended or revoked or renewals may be refused in such a way that the broadcaster will be ruined before he can have a day in court. A bill has been recently introduced in Congress to protect the independence of radio from bureaucratic absolutism. It will require the indignant support of the people to be enacted.

Following the German model of leaving business in private hands but taking away its management and profits, we have for comparison, in Germany, "the government does not put any maximum limit on the amount of profits that can be *earned*, but it prohibits *free use* of profits by providing that all joint stock companies which in the future distribute dividends exceeding 6 per cent . . . to pay the excess amount into a fund managed by the

Gold Discount Bank as trustee." (Economic Development of Germany Under National Socialism.) In the United States we saw a similar device in the undistributed profits tax.

In the field of actual management of business we have seen the recent instance of a great utility company deciding to issue $10,000,000 of its bonds to get new money *to put men to work* in plant expansion, and then seeing the Securities and Exchange Commission telling the Company it could not issue bonds, it must issue stock or nothing. So it issued nothing and no men were taken off relief rolls and put on the payrolls.

This act of tyranny had nothing to do with protecting the public against the sale of fraudulent securities. It was purely a determination of policy by an agency of government which had invested nothing in the business.

This is the way the Nazis operate. Only a lawyer, perhaps, can appreciate what a vital change of government attitude toward business is here involved. It is revolutionary in concept and will, unless stopped, be revolutionary in result. If SEC can override business management on a matter of this sort, it can with equal justice tell the business what it can use the money for, whether for plant expansion, or for gymnasiums and swimming pools for its employes, as is done in lands less happy than ours.

Heretofore the United States Supreme Court has held again and again that the federal government has no constitutional power to *manage* private enterprise. It can, within certain limits, *regulate* business when necessary in the public interest. In other words, it can say what business shall *not* do to prevent public injury. It cannot tell business what it *must* do as a matter of company policy.

That is what the United States Supreme Court *used* to hold. National Socialism marches on.

This assumption of managerial power by SEC is forcing business to by-pass it, if it legally can. Business is now selling whole security issues at private sale to single buyers such as insurance companies. This does not come under SEC control, as a public sale to many people does not take place. From $326,000,000 in 1935 private placement of securities grew to a total of $2,400,000,000 in 1939.

Undoubtedly, the bureaucracy will attempt to get further controls from Congress to prevent the by-pass. But the Republic suffers from all this. It fosters monopolies. Little companies, and new companies, like Henry Ford when he needed $28,000, are being squeezed out of the capital markets. The expense of SEC approval, if procured, places such a premium on the cost of money that they are frightened from organizing and expanding. But the established companies, the giants in the field, with powerful friends in the money markets, find ways and means.

And so the program fosters the very "concentration of capital" which the TNEC is so concerned about. But the whole thing is entirely logical from the standpoint of the socialist planners. They want business concentrated. It is then easier to take over.

7

FREEDOM OR FEUDALISM

"In passing by the side of Mount Thai, Confucius came on a woman who was weeping bitterly by a grave. The Master pressed forward and drove quickly to her; then he sent Tze-lu to question her. 'Your wailing,' said he, 'is that of one who has suffered sorrow on sorrow.' She replied, 'That is so. Once my husband's father was killed here by a tiger. My husband was also killed, and now my son has died in the same way.' The Master said, 'Why do you not leave the place?' The answer was, 'There is no oppressive government here.' The Master then said, 'Remember this, my children: Oppressive government is more terrible than tigers.'"

THERE ARE and always have been just two kinds of government—without the consent of the governed, and with the consent of the governed. Having suffered under the first, our fathers chose the second.

For a time the first may work fairly well. Under a good tyrant, such as Marcus Aurelius, men were perhaps better governed than they are under a corrupt machine in an American city where, in theory if not in fact, the people consent.

National Socialism *works* in Germany—so far. There is no doubt about it. At a price it can work anywhere, given leaders of undoubted capacity, such as Hitler and Goering. But the price must be paid. Part of it is the loss of liberty—"the one word, in every language, fit for the lips of a god." Another part is to pay for the mistakes and vices of those who rule.

63

When these appear the cost is very great. It is the difference between 130,000,000 men driving 30,000,000 automobiles, and one man driving one automobile loaded with 130,000,000 people. In the former the law of averages makes some mistakes and casualties certain. In the latter, there *may* be no mistake, but if you get a drunken driver, a whole nation may go to its doom, or a generation of young men to their graves.

In time you always get a drunken driver. Power is the most intoxicating wine man ever drank. Witness Napoleon wanting to put one of his brothers on every throne of Europe. And Alexander weeping because there were no more worlds to conquer. And Timurlane with his pyramid of skulls. And Hitler. And Stalin.

Our fathers knew that by an inner law of its own gravity power *always tends to abuse,* and the greater the power the greater the abuse. For the long pull they preferred the common denominator of the judgment of all, faulty as it may be, to the single judgment of one. They placed the pyramid of government upon the broad base of popular sovereignty, rather than upon the apex of one-man rule. They felt that the first pyramid has less chance of tipping over. They were willing to give great power to one man for a short time, as in war. But they never wanted the emergency of sudden necessity to become a precedent for permanent policy.

When our fathers wrote the Constitution of the United States they did something that had never happened before in the world. They did not transfer *total* power from one hand to many hands, from Moloch to Caesar to feudal lord to Demos. If they had done that we would have only the poor choice expressed by Voltaire when he said, "I had as lief be devoured by a single lion as by a hundred rats."

They did not do that. They did not place total power in their own hands or any of their agents. They did not choose to be ruled either by kings or by mobs. When they destroyed the Divine Right of Kings they did not set up the Divine Right of the Mob. Our fathers never confused themselves with God. "Vox populi vox dei"—the voice of the people is the voice of God—was not their conception of "democracy."

Other great charters, Magna Charta and the Bill of Rights, had placed limits upon the power of kings in whose elevation to the throne they had no voice. But our fathers placed limits upon their own selected agents. They even placed limits on their own people. They did not *wholly* trust *themselves*. They were humble men. What they did was something without precedent in all history. It was "the new order of the ages," Novus ordo seclorum, words which you will find inscribed on the Great Seal of your country reproduced on the back of the one dollar bill. It is worth your study.

The Constitution is the dyke our fathers erected against the tossing seas of despotic power, whether of dictators or mobs. It lodges supreme power nowhere. No one basket contains all the eggs. The men who wrote it knew that liberty is safe and the rights of man secure only when power is widely distributed, and never when it is concentrated. The checks and balances of the Constitution are to prevent any of their agents obtaining supreme power. They are to prevent totalitarian government. They brought an end to the idea that man is but a cell in the totality called the State, a species of human cattle to be ordered around by men with whips. They were the beginning of the Citizen. They said that the Citizen has certain *inalienable* rights which did not come from the State, which the State cannot lawfully take away, which the Citizen cannot rightfully vote away. They came from the Creator. The Citizen is the trustee of those *God-given* rights for himself and his posterity.

The Declaration of Independence and the Constitution of the United States are therefore the greatest liberal and liberating documents ever placed on parchment. They were not written by reactionaries, nor was the Revolution of 1776 fought by tories.

It is therefore one of the strangest lunacies of history that the men and women of both our great parties who now stand for the kind of government our fathers established are denounced as reactionaries, and those who would return to the concentrated political and economic power our fathers crossed the stormy North Atlantic to escape, are pleased to call themselves "liberals"!

"We have lived in an age so debauched from all humanity and reason that some stick not to turn butchers to their own privileges and conspirators against their own liberties," said William Penn in 1670 when on trial for speaking on London streets without permission.

"Conspirators against their own liberties!" Experience is a dear school but fools learn in no other, as Poor Richard says. The worst smoke screen of all is the one that blinds the eyes of those who started it.

I know the excuse these political sophomores give themselves. They say: We will concentrate not only political but economic power in Washington (or Berlin, or Rome, or Moscow). But we will retain *all* our civil rights!

These pundits may mean well, perhaps, but they haven't read history. Apparently they don't even read the newspapers!

What civil rights did anybody have in Louisiana under the reign of Huey I, our first dictator? And what civil rights has anyone in Italy, Russia, Germany? Men are green in judgment when they suppose that supreme power will permit itself to be challenged by opposition parties, that it will permit its sweet perquisites to be whittled away by free speech, free press, free elections, labor organizations, even by pastor or priest.

Bertrand Russell is a socialist. But he is apparently intellectually honest. In his last book "Power," he confesses his dilemma. He advocates "State ownership of land and capital." But he knows "how rash it is to expect irresponsible power to be benevolent." He sees the inevitable danger that those who seek liberation from economic tyranny will find that "they have *inadvertently* established a new tyranny *at once economic and political,* more drastic and more terrible than any previously known."

And so he is troubled. He *hopes* that with the government owning all capital—for example, the newspapers—it would still be so kind as to *permit* the opposition to have one page to attack it! He should submit this to Adolph, Jozef and Co.!

Of course, if Bertrand Russell and his comrades of the "intelligentsia" were to solve the knotty problem of chaining two tigers (economic and political power combined) when they find difficulty in chaining one separately, we would still disagree as to their main theme—State ownership as in Russia, or State management as in Germany. Free men do more and better work than slaves. Logic says so, and the records prove it. The hope of reward as a greater stimulus to individual effort has not since Jefferson's day been a mere theory. America is the proof.

Why *is* this country the greatest in the world? Three reasons, chiefly: One, the natural resources of sun and soil and the treasure beneath the soil; two, the character of our people. Since Plymouth Rock down to the mother and father of Colonel Charles A. Lindbergh a continuing process has gone on. By and large it was the strong and daring who braved the Atlantic to conquer the wilderness of the

West. The timid and weak stayed in their overseas homes. Three, the Constitution of the United States which freed men from too much and too costly a government—"Swarms of officers to eat out our substance," as the Declaration of Independence put it—and guaranteed that they could keep what they honestly made.

Let us go back to the beginning of our free institutions.

It has been forgotten that the 101 pioneers who came over in the Mayflower set up a socialistic commonwealth, somewhat like Brook Farm or New Harmony of grandfather's time, or the Tugwelltowns of today. No one was "to have and to hold" the fruit of his own toil. All was to go into the common store. Those who fished, hunted, farmed, or felled the tall timber, were to throw their fish, deer, vegetables and lumber into a single heap from which all might share equally. Under this system the drone got as much as the worker—or putting it another way, the worker got no more than the drone.

No doubt this in part was due to the necessities of their situation. Common perils compelled a common defense and a mutual protection. Other perils today produce somewhat similar socialistic mechanisms, such as the navy or the fire department. But as a means to encourage the production of new wealth, how did the Pilgrims' planned economy succeed?

In 1621 and 1622 they continued to struggle along with immense fortitude, but heartbreaking results. But in the third year, 1623, in the words of the old chronicle, "God gave them plenty, and the face of things was changed to the rejoicing of hearts." In that year they had changed from Socialism to a system "in which a stimulus of individual interest quickened the alacrity of toil." To each family was given the use of a separate parcel of land. This "made all hands very industrious so as much more corn was planted than otherwise would have been, and it gave far better content. The women went willingly into the field and took their little ones with them to set the corn, whom to have compelled would have been thought great oppression."

These quaint words from a chronicle of the times record the beginning of free enterprise in America. And it was that autumn that William Bradford, "Ye Governor of Ye Colony," issued the first Thanksgiving proclamation. He asked the Pilgrims "to gather at ye meethouse on ye hill" and there thank the "Great Father" not only for such natural resources as the game in the forest, and the fish and clams of the sea, but for "an abundant harvest of Indian corn, wheat, peas, beans, squashes and garden vegetables" —all new wealth produced by human effort.

It is noteworthy that our pioneer forbears abandoned 317 years ago the very system to which Socialists, Communists and Fascists are now urging us to return. They did so not because someone wrote "Das Kapital" nor because of a blueprint or diagram drawn in an attic. They did so as the result of bitter experience on a stern and rockbound coast. They learned from life itself. They learned what we are now being urged to forget—that the reward of individual toil is the best assurance of enough "plenty" to have a Thanksgiving worth celebrating.

And by the time gold was discovered in California in 1849, the thrifty sons and daughters of the Pilgrims of Massachusetts alone, a State with no minerals, coal, or petroleum, and with a scanty soil, had created and saved under this system of free enterprise for the profit motive, enough new wealth so that they "could have given a dollar to each individual of the one thousand millions of the inhabitants of the earth, and still have all their schools, meetinghouses, town houses, almshouses, gaols, and literary and benevolent institutions left as nest eggs to begin the world anew."

There is no greater perversion of political terms than that those who believe in the free enterprise system which "changed the face of things" 317 years ago are now called "reactionaries" and those who would now go back to the system the Pilgrims abandoned now label themselves "liberals," applying "new remedies to modern needs"! "Give us power," they say, "and we will solve your problems for you."

Well, the promissory notes of the Socialist authoritarians are coming up for protest. With more power than has been entrusted to man in the western world for generations, we have today a shrinking prosperity and less stability, less security, less of freedom and the Rights of Man than has been known for decades.

Despite the glowing promises of these world-shakers, these men of blood and iron, these madmen hearing voices in the air, what is the result of all these tragic years? It is a mirage, a will o' the wisp. "Follow me. Behind the concentration camps of peace and the cemeteries of war there is the Promised Land!"

It has always been a mystery to me how we got to be the greatest, the richest and the happiest nation in the world today by doing everything wrong!

8

THEY LET THE TOWN HALL BURN

A SON CAME home from college. He said, "Father, I hate to tell you this, but I've become a socialist." His father said, "That's all right, son. You know when I got through school thirty years ago I said the same thing to your grandfather. But something happened that summer. We were all at the town hall one evening when a house caught fire and with a fierce gale blowing it looked as if it would clean out the whole village. Well, son, a curious thing happened. I noticed that everybody rushed home to save his own house and they let the town hall burn!"

St. Paul did not say, "Hold fast to everything." He knew the world changes and that it must from time to time put wornout things in its attic. But he did say, "Hold fast to that which *is* good." Well, that seems sensible. Why throw away something good simply because it is old?

I hope the day may soon come when every man who is willing to work may have for himself and his family a home of his own and a garden with hollyhocks along the wall, and a place for his children to play in the sun. And enough saved and safe to provide for "the years of the locust."

And because we want just that, we want to help restore and preserve freedom, economic and political, "to ourselves and our posterity."

71

"I have but one lamp by which my feet are guided, and that is the lamp of experience," said Patrick Henry. And so "let's look at the record."

If all the gold annually produced in the United States were divided equally among all our men; and all gold produced outside the United States were divided equally among its men, and two men, an American and a non-American, came together to talk about the different forms of government in the world, and how unhappy they were under all the different kinds, each bringing with him his share of gold, what would be the proportion of gold which the American and the non-American would have?

The American, 97%; the foreigner, 3%; and in the same way for other useful things produced or in use in America:

	American Per Cent	Foreigner Per Cent
Wheat	74	26
Butter	81	19
Milk	83	17
Coal	86	14
Cotton	93	7
Petroleum	96	4
Telephones	94	6
Aluminum	82	18
Cement	83	17
Silver	83	17
Tobacco	86	14
Rayon	87	13
Steel	90	10
Movie shows	91	9
Telephone calls	94	6
Automobiles	96	4
Railroad mileage	86	14
Improved highway mileage	88	12
Radios	94	6
Bathtubs	98	2
Civilian airplanes	97	3

There are, for example, more telephones in New York City, than in all Asia, with a billion people. But let us omit the three-quarters of the world's people who live in

Africa and Asia. Let us compare the United States, still
chiefly under free enterprise, with the second greatest land
power in the world—Germany, under National Socialism.
The comparison could be made before the world war, under the Kaiser, which would eliminate the question of her
war losses, debt, indemnities, etc. Or under Hitler, giving
him and his form of government the advantage of its supposed efficiency, its iron discipline, greater than the Kaiser's, its contempt for democracy, its debts nearly all wiped
out by repudiation (reduced from 179 billion reichmarks
in 1919 to 19 billions in 1929), and so starting with a clean
slate, its inherent capacity for honest administration (far
beyond us with the spoils system in our blood), its relative
freedom from crime, its docile people, its homogeneous
population, its century old traditions, its state religion
and the science, technology, research, patience, grit, and
willingness to work of a truly great people. Whether before or since the world war, the advantage would be on the
side of free enterprise.

Let us take National Socialism as it is. Let us measure
it by the yardstick of government as laid down in the Federalist Papers—"The public good, the real welfare of the
great body of the people, is the supreme object to be pur-
sued, and no form of government whatever has any other
value than as it may be fitted to the attainment of this
object."

Both Germany and the United States touched low in
1932. 1937 was the best year since then in both countries.
In the same currency (dollars) we had a national income
of $69,419,000,000; Germany, $28,534,000,000. But as
we had more people we must divide national income into
per capita figures. Per capita, American income was
$537; German income, $421.

(Detour: We have heard much about Sweden—"The
Middle Way"—the halfway house between free enterprise

and state control. The per capita income in Sweden in
1937 was $350, or only two-thirds as good as ours.)

In 1938 we almost equalled Germany in per capita taxes
—$108 to $110. In per cent of taxes taken from national
income in 1938, we showed 23.2%; Germany, 26.2, giving
her politicians a slightly larger fraction of the nation's
wealth to demonstrate the glories of National Socialism
than ours had. As against this, however, it must be stated
that we increased our debt and mortgaged our future
faster and heavier than did Germany.

Let us compare the United States, whose enterprise is
still predominately free, and Germany, where politicians
control nearly every decision. For the year 1936 we find:

	United States	*Germany*
Oil, per capita	425.0 gal.	2.5 gal.
KW of electricity	900	550
Death rate in first year	1 in 13	1 in 17
Wheat per capita	4.8 bu.	2.5 bu.
Wool per capita	3.5 lbs.	.6 lb.
Coal per capita	3.7 tons	2.6 tons
Steel per capita	417.0 lbs.	314.0 lbs.
Copper per capita	10.0 lbs.	1.0 lbs.
Pig Iron per capita	542 lbs.	502 lbs.
Bank deposits per capita	423 dollars (1937)	89 dollars (1935)
Automobile production	4,454,115	297,512
Miles of telephone wire	86,800,000	15,785,007
Books in public libraries	100,470,215	10,502,467
Students in college	1,250,000	68,148
Movie theatres	14,500	4,800
Doctors	1 for 765 persons	1 for 1,180 persons

For the Nazi hausfrau labor saving devices are a scarce
luxury. Electric refrigerators, vacuum sweepers, electric
irons, washing machines, sewing machines, toasters, etc.,
are practically unknown.

So much for the creature comforts of life. But man
lives not by bread alone. As the Super State has extended
its control over human lives what do we find: We find a
barrack room civilization.

We see one-party rule crushing all opposition; 1,000

newspapers abolished, all others State controlled; the
radio and movie State dominated; the Church in handcuffs; all education regimented from the kindergarten to
the University; labor unions destroyed, their treasuries
confiscated; the health of her people cracking under the
intense Spartan discipline and the neglect of political doc-
tors; the lawyer no longer free to defend his client, but
under a greater obligation to the State; the courts packed;
justice the tool of the party boss; hours of work lengthened; wages decreased; strikes abolished; credit in the
hands of the State; insurance largely run by the politicians; freedom to marry restricted; illegitimacy made
honorable; science, art, music and the theatre prostituted
to the preconceived notions of party and race; bachelors
taxed to procreate "cannon fodder," yet childless mar-
riages increasing, marking a silent rebellion; every alleged
father made responsible for bastard children; compulsory
labor service (serfdom to the State); "Hitler elections"
99 per cent pure; public office made the privilege of a new
caste; religion paganized. "The Prussian soldier is the
primal cell for the building of our complete being. . . .
We seek the total destruction of dishonorable democracy
which ignores the foundations of race"; the party line,
which is the discipline of the army, carried into civil life.

We see women again thrust back to Kirche, Kueche,
Kinder (Church, Kitchen, Children); criminal punishment not only for defined offenses but "for acts which de-
serve punishment according to the sound conception of
the people," i.e., government by the tyranny of men, not
by the rule of law; ex post facto justice, i.e., punishment
for an act not a crime when done; arrest without warrant
and imprisonment without trial; search and seizure at any
time and for no stated reason; no independent jury system; and finally the Gestapo and political murder.

Such is the modern Sparta. Now that it is seven years

old, the leaders boast that it will "last a thousand years."
But where is the old Laconia? And what monuments has
she left? None! Nothing but the record of "her laws and
her soldiers."

Seven years is a short yardstick. But can it be that
dictators make no mistakes, that it is only republics that
err? Where is this boasted efficiency of concentrated
power? Has Washington, D. C., made no mistakes?

Why did we have the 1937 crash? In his budget message of January, 1940, President Roosevelt said with great
candor, "The recession was due to a variety of causes stem-
ming *in the main* from over-optimism which led *the government* to curtail its net expenditures too sharply." So
the *government* brought on hard times! Meaning well,
it did ill—another proof of "the harm that good men do."
When the kindhearted druggist by mistake puts poison in
the bottle, just what good is the fact that he "meant well"
(and "tried hard")? Assuming that Mr. Roosevelt correctly diagnosed his mistake, is it assumed that he or other
presidents will never make other mistakes costing billions?

The fact is that an imposing case can be made for the
proposition that most of our troubles since the world war
ended (if not our participation in that war) have been due
to government mismanagement and official bungling—
post war tariffs of 1922–29; I.C.C. handcuffs on railroads;
economic planning by the Federal Reserve board, squeez-
ing credit in 1921 and inflating it in 1927–29; foreign
loans; stock market Pollyannaism by government officials; and beginning in 1928 bootstrap government of cotton, pricing it out of the world market for which the penalty will not be paid for fifty years. Both parties have
been at fault in this "planning" business.

Capitalism has serious evils mixed with its enormous
good. But what do men mean when they say they are

"against" capitalism? Do they abolish capitalism by adopting communism or fascism? They simply transfer the capital to the State. Russia is a capitalistic country. It has railroads, factories, farms, capital, has it not? Will her capital be more wisely and justly administered by politicians who can hide their blunders and charge their deficits to the taxpayers? Who have nothing of their own to lose and no reward of their own to gain except place or power or graft?

Strange it is that this modern tendency to render all things to Caesar—education, hospitals, the care of the sick, the errands of mercy, the compassion of suffering, the support and therefore the slavery of the church through public taxation, the destruction of local self government, the bribery of states, the pressure for the control of radio, the press and lecture rooms, the justification given for diverting huge public funds to tons of propaganda, the sneers at the Constitution and the courts, the most disinterested interpreters of its meaning, and the most independent guardians of your inalienable rights, the gradual erosion of the sense of personal responsibility for the care of one's aged parent, one's child, one's community and its charities and philanthropies—strange it is, that all this has been so successfully sold to so many people as a progressive and liberal movement. It is a false label for spurious goods. Hidden within the velvet glove of much so-called "social welfare" is the iron hand of Caesar. We are voting God out of office!

Strange it is that after seeing enormous tolls collected from the lesser businesses of liquor, race tracks, dance halls, red light districts, prize fighting, wrestling, slot machines, road building, municipal supplies, even school books for our children, that we should hanker and yearn to turn over all business, all trade, all treasure, transportation, banking, mining, commerce and industry to the modern Caesars, their courtiers, their courtesans and their soldiers.

There are always two dangers in making political appraisal. Each is exaggeration, one on the plus, the other on the minus side. "We point with pride—we view with alarm!"

We are yet a long way from National Socialism of the Hitler species. We will probably *never* get that variety. But that we are moving *toward* some form of National Socialism and *away from* our form of government seems hard to not believe.

"Men have been sometime led by degrees, sometimes hurried into things of which, *if they could have seen the whole together*, they never would have permitted the most remote approach,"

said Edmund Burke, friend of America.

"The apparent enthusiasm for the manual worker, for the afflicted, and for social justice, *serves as a mask* (smoke-screen) to facilitate the refusal of all obligations,"

says Ortega Y. Gassett.

"A dangerous ambition more often lurks behind the *specious mask* of zeal for the rights of the people than under the forbidding appearance of zeal for the firmness and efficiency of government. History will teach us that the former has been found a much more certain road to the introduction of despotism than the latter, and that of those men who have overturned the liberties of republics, the greatest number have begun their career by paying an obsequious court to the people; commencing demagogues, and ending tyrants."—No. 1 of the Federalist Papers.

"The spirit of encroachment tends to consolidate the powers of all the departments in one, and thus create, whatever *form* of government, *a real despotism*. A just estimate of that love of power, and proneness to abuse it, which predominates in the human heart, is sufficient to satisfy us of the truth of this position. The necessity of reciprocal checks in the exercise of political power, by dividing and distributing it into different depositories, and constituting each the Guardian of the Public Weal, against invasions by others, has been evinced by experiments, ancient and modern; *some of them in our country and under our own eyes.* To preserve them must be as necessary as to institute them."—Washington's Farewell Address.

What is really at stake in America today is *our form of government.* The issue is Freedom or Feudalism.

* * * * * * *

"If those changes come which will make our cause a more defensible one, we shall not only have the strength of justice, but shall perhaps have moved so far toward those ideals which communist believers also share, that *no resort to force may be necessary.* . . . Every student who is interested in peace (Finland!), prosperity and progress must, in the coming years, devote much study and thought to Russia and the Russians."—Rexford Guy Tugwell in American Economic Life.

9

BALANCE SHEET

JIM MADDEN, breeder of race horses, was once asked: "In your opinion, what horse was the greatest sire of the American turf?" His answer was, "Opinions are worthless. It is only the records that stand."

The record of the past seven years is both good and bad. Jeffersonian democracy has been mixed with the "New Deal." The latter, in its now disclosed direction, is Big Government, the dinosaur Jefferson and all genuine liberals have fought since Hobbes wrote "The Leviathan" 300 years ago—and before.

It is hard to appraise the balance sheet of seven years. Men and accountants differ as to whether this item or that is plus or minus.

But on the asset side, and with some qualifications, it seems to me that we must put:

The divorcement of commercial and investment banking
The guaranty of bank deposits
The regulation of stock exchanges
The regulation of the interstate sale of securities
The growth of national income from $42 to $68 billions
Reciprocal trade agreements, on net balance more gain than loss
Part of the public utility bill
The Lindbergh Act and the war on kidnapping
The CCC Camps
Much of the PWA program

Soil conservation
The handling of foreign affairs, and national defense
The recognition of the right of collective bargaining
Home Owners Loan Corporation
Federal Housing Administration
Relief—but badly managed
Civil Aeronautics Administration
Pure Food and Drug Amendments
Truck and bus legislation

Most of these items come within the Jeffersonian principle—"prevent men from injuring one another." This is as old as the common law. Centuries ago it was the law that if a man digs an excavation he must shore up his neighbor's wall. He is not permitted to invade, defraud, or exploit those who are weaker or who have the right to rely on honest dealing. And the relief of distress is as old as Christian charity.

The fact that some of these items have taken the federal government into new fields does not disturb me, where it is the only power capable of dealing with the problem. For example, the regulation of air transportation.

On the debit side I put items both accomplished as well as desired but defeated:

The Supreme Court packing bill
The Reorganization bill of 1938
The Lend-spend bill of 1939
The "death sentence" in the Utility bill. This was government by meat axe
The "purge"
The fanning of class hatred
Attitude toward sit down strikes
The fascistic administration of SEC
A direct debt of $42 billions, and billions more, indirect, threatening inflation, or repudiation
The liquidation of thrift, and the war on savings, through enforced low interest rates
Eight million still unemployed

The development of the "corporative state," or cartels by
nationwide closed shop industrial bargaining units, as in coal,
creating industrial and labor monopolies

Infringement upon the right to work

NLRB favoritism and tyranny

The belittlement of the press

The "invisible government" of radio

The development of "equal privileges for all" rather than
war against all privilege

The use of relief funds, public work and subsidy payments
to corrupt the ballot, thus invading the greatest civil right of
all, a free election

Government competition with banking, except when impera-
tively necessary, and to cease thereafter

The foreign silver buying policy

Undistributed profits tax

Tax rates so high they discourage enterprise

Bureaucratic growth, waste and absolutism

The continued invasion of states rights

The "legalized embezzlement" in social security, and a pay
roll tax that will either be so high as to strangle business, or so
low as to make government insurance insolvent

The development of the "Papa State" philosophy atrophying
the spiritual sinews of our people

Fostering the false theory that government can "create" pur-
chasing power. It can, as an heir borrows against his inheritance

Too much emphasis on consumers goods, at the expense of
capital goods

The doctrine that America is built—defeatism. Policy
hitched to the philosophy of scarcity

The United States Housing Administration and various
"Tugwelltowns" subsidized by taxation. Slum clearance is a
state or local problem

TVA—beyond flood control and the development of waterways. The rest of the program should have been contracted to
private industry

A Nine Billion Dollar budget now glorified as an "investment" with seven consecutive annual deficits and no end in
sight, constituting a threat against savings, and a brake on
progress

A Pink and Red strain in government with evident hostility

toward free enterprise, and a constant, though camouflaged, march toward National Socialism

The concentration of huge discretionary power in the Executive

NRA [1]

Wage-Hour: Wages, yes; hours, no. Hours should be left to state law

Guffey Coal bill

Placing reform ahead of recovery after the Roy Howard letter in September, 1935

The progressive freezing of our economy by inflexible costs, supported or imposed by government

National and farm income far below the point to which they should have risen

The loss of cotton export markets

Neglect of our railroad problem

Constant unpredictability of policy

Building "new instruments of public power" which in other hands "would provide shackles for the liberties of the people"

Many plus or minus points will occur to the reader, omitted above. And there will be disagreement as to the inclusion of various items or on which side of the balance

---

[1] NRA codes were a close approach to the "corporative state" of Italian fascism. "I have learned from Roosevelt and from Stalin," Signor Mussolini told a representative of the Echo de Paris in the autumn of 1933, when NRA was going into action. (The New Deal in Europe—Emil Lengyel.)

Many NRA codes adopted the principle of the European cartel. They undertook to monopolize and apportion the market among themselves by freezing out competitors. For example, in the furniture code no new furniture factory could be built unless permission were granted.

For a parallel see *The Third Reich,* by Henri Lichtenberger, p. 251:

"Not only has the state not given way to private initiative but it closely supervises private enterprise and often suppresses it. In certain industries like potash and textiles, for example, it has gone so far as to forbid new installations. Since it reserves for itself the right to put capital in circulation, it also decides in what manner the available capital shall be used."

It was of NRA that President Roosevelt said:

"History probably will record the National Industrial Recovery Act as the most important and far reaching legislation ever enacted by an American Congress."

sheet to put them. The problem is: On net balance, is the government's program in the black or in the red? Or perhaps the question might be stated: Has the program now given us, and which its logical sequence will give us, the present and long range prosperity, security and happiness we reasonably had the right to expect?

As a lifelong Democrat who never voted any other national or state ticket and as a loyal supporter of the New Deal as I understood it in 1932, I regret to say that on the testimony of trustworthy witnesses, partial to the administration, the verdict must be, No.

First Witness: President Roosevelt:

"A major problem of your Committee will be to ascertain why a large part of our vast reservoir of money and savings have remained idle in stagnant pools. . . . I know of no more urgent question in the country today." (Letter to Senator Joseph O'Mahoney, May 16, 1939.)

Second Witness: John L. Lewis:

"As the current year opens, the Democratic Party is in default to the American people. After 7 years of power, it finds itself without solution for the major questions of unemployment, low national income, mounting internal debt, increasing direct and consumer taxation, and restricted foreign markets. There still exists the same national unhappiness that it faced 7 years ago. Labor and the people are losing confidence.

It was, if the United States Supreme Court, by an unanimous opinion, had not ruled that it was outside our system of constitutional government. For this and other opinions the Court was charged by Attorney General Robert Jackson as having cancelled out Mr. Roosevelt's first term.

It is not to be forgotten, however, that important American business men sponsored the NRA in the same way that their European colleagues, men like the fugitive August Thyssen, got behind the Socialists Mussolini and Hitler in their climb to power. What they *wanted* was a dictator who would dictate to their competitors and to their workingmen. What they *got* was a dictator who dictated to *them*.

"It is not my fault if these men took me for a simpleton and found afterwards that it was they who had been fooled," said Herr Hitler. (The Voice of Destruction—Hermann Rauschnig.)

They fear for the future, and rightly so." Address to the United Mine Workers of America Convention at Columbus, Ohio, January 24, 1940.

Third Witness: the American Federation of Labor:

"Unemployment still is the most acute domestic problem of the Nation. No orderly and intelligent effort has yet been made to determine the facts with regard to its causes, its extent, its cure. As a nation we have not hesitated to spend billions for the relief of those who are unemployed, but we have neglected to take the necessary steps to reduce and end unemployment. At this time there are not enough jobs in private industry to go around. This is largely due, in our opinion, to the fact that lack of confidence has stunted business growth and expansion. We demand that those in authority take whatever steps may be necessary to restore business confidence. We urge that all Government actions that tend unnecessarily to discourage business expansion cease and that a positive effort be made to encourage greater industrial activity. We have learned the lesson that when opportunities for profit diminish opportunities for jobs likewise disappear."—The executive council of the American Federation of Labor, Miami, Fla., Jan. 31, 1940.

The last statement of the third witness is particularly terse. It recognizes that American business is a three-legged stool, and stands, if it stands at all, only on all three legs—Men, Money and Management. Government helps neither of any two legs (nor itself, as the silent tax partner sitting on the stool) by sawing off the third leg.

Other testimony, not biased by American political opinion, is world recovery in relation to our own. All charts show that both world and American industrial production touched bottom in 1932.[2] With Russian figures unavail-

---

[2] We are now referring to per cent of recovery since 1932. These figures do not mean that the average American citizen is worse off than citizens of other countries. He is better off. He always has been better off with a higher per capita income. Even in 1932 he was better off. But relatively to the low point of the depression we have recovered less rapidly than the other great nations of the world.

able, we compare our per cent of recovery with that of 16
other leading nations:

In March, 1936, we were in 13th place.
In August, 1937, we were in 11th place.
In February, 1938, we were in 17th place.
In December, 1939, we were in 17th place.

Just before the outbreak of war in September, 1939, we
were almost back to 1923–24–25 in the production of industrial goods (102) whereas world figures were 161.

In 1937, our best year, with 1923–24–25 = 100, we were
at 110; the world at 114.

*In no year or month since 1932 has our recovery
equalled world recovery.* The closest approach was in
early 1933. This was while we were still operating as Jeffersonian Democrats.

Compared with the low point of the depression we have
made progress. But relatively to the rest of the world we
are close to the foot of the class.

For the first time since Jamestown and Plymouth Rock
we have lived ten years without equalling and surpassing
our previous peak.

When our possibilities are compared to that of the
world's the comparison is still less to our credit. Our ter-
ritory had not been overrun by soldiers, as in France; our
merchant fleet had not been sunk, as in England; crushing
indemnities had not been imposed on us, as in Germany;
we had not lost 8,500,000 of our best young men, as had
Europe; we had a friendlier climate than Canada or Sweden, or Chile; we had more than half the gold in the world,
now two-thirds; protected by two oceans, we were more
nearly self sustaining than any great nation except Russia; we had the most skilled labor, the highest technology;
the best transportation system; the finest schools; the
smallest standing army, one of the lowest dead weights of

armament; no international debt. Yet with these un-
equalled advantages we constantly have lagged behind almost every nation in the world.

Such is the dispassionate record. Our effort to "remake
the world" has been something less than a complete suc-
cess.

Other indices, on the whole, reinforce this conclusion.
In the four Hoover years, 1928–1932, inclusive, national
income produced averaged $60.8 billions; in the six New
Deal years, 1933–1938, it averaged $57.6 billions. On a
per capita basis, income in Hoover's four years averaged
$507; in the six New Deal years, $452, or 10 per cent less.

Other facts to be considered are increase of population,
taxes, debt and cost of living. In the New Deal years the
government took from a smaller income a larger tax by a
billion dollars a year, and increased the debt 3 billions a
year.

One point in favor of the New Deal years is that the
cost of living averaged 75.5 as against 80 under Mr. Hoover. The Roosevelt dollar bought somewhat more goods
than the Hoover dollar. But against this is the higher tax
and the debt charged against future income.

The Hoover years were nothing to brag about. But it
must be a sobering thought to sincere New Dealers that
the Roosevelt years have not equalled them.

But let us omit the Hoover years, 1929 boom, 1932 bust.
Let us compare the "par" period of 1923–24–25 with 1939,
just finished, war bulge and all. 1923–24–25 has been
adopted by government agencies as "par." It was neither
boom nor bust. It followed the post-war period of 1921
when industrial production almost touched the 1932 low,
and preceded by 6 to 4 years the skyrocket year of 1929.

We have been "shooting for par." What's the score?

In 1939 the Department of Commerce estimates national income produced (total value of all goods and serv-

ices) at $68.5 billions. In the three par years, 1923–24–25,
it was $71.6 billions, or nearly three billions more at a time
when taxes and debt were being reduced, not increased.

But if 1923–24–25 was par = 100, then 1939 ought to be
114 because we now have 114 people to divide our income
among as against 100 people then. In other words, we
should now have an income of $81.6 billions at least, to
have the same per capita income now as then. Instead,
we had $68.5 billions in 1939, or $13.1 billions less, on a
population basis, than we had 17–15 years ago. At an estimated population in 1939 of 131,000,000, per capita income averaged $523. At an estimated population in the
par period of 113,500,000, per capita income averaged $630.

In short, man for man, we were $107 worse off in dollar
income in 1939 than in 1923–24–25. We have not even
stood still. We have gone back. Our retrogression is offset in part by the lower cost of living in 1939, but the
higher taxes and future debt are counterbalances against
this saving. The national debt in the par period averaged
about $21,300,000,000. On June 30, 1939, it was $40,439,-
000,000 (not counting contingent liabilities of $5,469,000,-
000), or $19,139,000,000 more. Per capita the debt today
is $147 greater than in 1934.

The industrial worker who has steady work the year
through is undoubtedly better off due to higher wage rates
and shorter hours. But the part time employed, and the
unemployed are certainly worse off. Practically speaking
few who wanted to work in 1923–25 were without a job.
In only twelve months in the past seven years has total
factory employment and pay rolls been above 1923–25.
The farmer is considerably worse off. In 1939 cash farm
income, including subsidies, was $7,625,000,000. In
1923–25 it averaged $9,675,000,000, or more than $2 billion
more. And all persons dependent on interest, dividends,
pensions, annuities, insurance, rents—the old people, in

short—are in much more straitened circumstances. It is certainly true, also, that young people, 18 to 25 or 30, are worse off.

Privately endowed institutions—schools, colleges, churches, missions, hospitals, medical research, foundations, trusts, Y.M.C.A's, etc., have lost, according to the president of Amherst College, one-third of their endowment income, due to artificially produced shrinkage of earnings. In addition, the rapidly increasing taxes on inheritance are reducing the number and amount of gifts from philanthropic men and women. As the sources of their revenues continue to dry up, these institutions are faced with the necessity of curtailing their service, or leaning upon the State for support. The danger that threatens them is a major public concern when it is remembered that democracy is the child of the Christian religion, not the progeny of Caesar. The separation of State and Church, and the independence of the latter, is basic to our institutions. If the State becomes the receiver in bankruptcy of the Church and Christian charity, it will be a solar plexus blow.

"We test what we have done as our measures take root in the living texture of life," said President Roosevelt in his annual message to Congress in January, 1935. What he actually meant by "the new economic order rising from the disintegration of the old" which he referred to at that time has never been entirely clear. Despite the fairly legible totalitarian blue prints of Tugwell, Berle, Saposs, Madden, Hopkins and others less candid, I have never felt —do not now feel—that Mr. Roosevelt intended a bad result. Nor do I think Hitler or Mussolini intend a bad result. Mr. Roosevelt took over a broken down machine and with great courage attempted, at first, to repair it. But under the psychology of the times and the pressure of events, emergency measures lengthened out, perhaps with-

out fully conscious design, into permanent policies at war
with the American tradition. Starting as a professed Jeffersonian he has emerged far beyond Alexander Hamilton.

Why, then, 8,000,000 unemployed in the richest country in the world as we still struggle for recovery, in the
11th year since the Great Wind of 1929?

Economic nationalism and a gradually closing world
economy have admittedly added to our difficulties as a
long time exporting nation, although, as previously stated,
the world has recovered from the valley of 1932 faster and
more than we.

But on our own side of the Atlantic what domestic reasons exist?

Has it been due to the machine—technological unemployment? At one time I gave this a position of importance, but I now think I was in error. The machine destroys jobs, it is true, but it also creates them through
lower costs, increasing sales and broadening markets. On
net balance, it seems certain that the machine creates more
jobs than it destroys. As the axe to the frontiersman, the
net to the fisherman, the plow in place of the crooked stick,
the mine hoist in place of the backs of mules or children,
the machinery of peace cannot be considered the enemy of
man.

Was it because capital wilfully hoarded its gold? No.
The fact is that American business management paid out
of accumulated surplus during the depression not less than
$13.5 billion dollars.

Was it due to over-production? No. In a land that has
had and still has a greater diffusion of the necessities and
comforts of living than any other on God's footstool, there
are still 80 per cent who have never enjoyed the standard
of living they would like to have or which would insure
the health and happiness which this Great Age could produce.

Was it because American labor soldiered on the job?
No. All things considered American labor has been mar-
vellously patient and magnificently patriotic. During the
worst year of 1932 the employed workman turned out
more work per man than ever in history.

What then is the answer?

In my judgment, Cold Feet and Hothouse Statesmen,
seeking the Millennium Tomorrow. The Cold Feet were
caused by the policies previously discussed, government
competition, excessive spending, too high taxes, doubt as
to the real goal of government, confusion of policy, hostility to free enterprise, the detour from the American
way, the concentration of power, depending on the exercise of unpredictable discretion, bureaucratic tyrannies.
"We must allow for some play in the joints of the machine," said Justice Oliver Wendell Holmes. Wise man.

At this point I quote Wendell L. Willkie, one time Hoo-
sier Democrat, and a two fisted fighting man who hits only
above the belt, where he hits them hard. At Toledo, Ohio,
March 4, 1940, he recalled the false prosperity of the
1920s,

"when business men, drunk with power, and a public drunk
with money destroyed the safeguards which protected individual liberties. For awhile I hoped that the New Deal would
replace it with a truly liberal faith. Certainly, no liberal
movement ever had a greater opportunity, or was ever given
more whole-hearted support by the people. But the leaders
seemed to be motivated not by love, but by hate; they preferred to punish rather than reform; they wanted to destroy
the evil doers, even if the doers of good should also succumb.

"For a time this lack of discrimination puzzled many of us,
but it is puzzling us no longer. Its explanation is found in the
fact that the purpose of this new government was not to eliminate monopolistic control, but its ownership. Today it is not
big business that we have to fear. It is big government. The
abuses that corrupted the 1920s have been transferred from
Wall Street to Washington.

"Recall to your mind, for a moment, the abuses charged against business in the twenties. The first was the concentration of excessive power in the hands of a few men; second, the use of this power and the money that went with it to influence political decisions; third, the manipulation of financial markets to the detriment of the investors and enrichment of the manipulator; fourth, the ruthless determination to destroy opposition and create a monopoly. Every one of these abuses exists today. We can repeat each one of those accusations. But the responsible party today is not the nation's business, but the nation's government.

"For example, on the first point, never before has this country experienced so extraordinary a concentration of power in the hands of a few men as in the government today. All of the safeguards erected by the American people against too autocratic a government have been invaded.

"We have grown so hardened to the concentration of power in the hands of the executive department that we read, day after day, without a quiver, newspaper paragraphs discussing whether or not the President has decided to encourage private enterprise or whether he will continue the government's vast spend-lend program to add to the deficit and further delay investment confidence.

"It is no longer news that the decision of one man should determine the direction in which this country will move.

"This concentration of political power in the hands of a few men not controlled by the people is just as bad as the concentration of economic power in the twenties; and it leads as rapidly to the second abuse of which business was accused a decade ago; namely, the use of this power to influence political decisions."

In closing I repeat what I wrote in "Jefferson, The Forgotten Man." I say it as one who has always fought the evils of concentrated economic control over the lives of Americans:

"Big Government is a poor alternative to Big Business. In fact, if the only alternative to economic autocracy were a political autocracy, I would prefer the former. I might be its wage slave, but as long as my government is free, and my newspaper is free, and the ballot box is open, and my vote is counted, and the judge on the bench is beyond control, I can fight for my freedom and struggle against my fate.

"But under a political autocracy, all weapons of defense are taken away. Economic destiny is dictated by government, and protests are answered with guns. When government becomes guardian, the very necessity to make its program succeed means the end of civil rights. What are civil rights, *They are rights against government*.

"Even religion, which is based upon the dignity of man as a child of God, is considered, and rightly so, the enemy of the authoritarian state. Mussolini, for example, says that Italians must be Fascists, that is, party members, before they are Catholics. In Germany the Hohenzollern said, 'Me and God'; Hitler says 'Me or God.' They call this progress!

"One of the most dangerous elements involved in teaching people to look to government for salvation is that government will be held responsible for its promises. If, which God forbid, there be another crash like 1929, it will be Washington, D. C., and not Wall Street that will get the blame.

" 'Economic Royalists' will be glad that the blame has been shifted from them, but it will be a sad day for democracy. Then, as always, the old excuse will be made, that the failure was due to insufficient power, and a new crisis psychology will call for the Strong Man himself, who thrice declining the crown at last permits duty to overcome modesty! Such is the pathology of republics.

"The problem was correctly stated by President Roosevelt at the beginning, 'to reverse the process of the concentration of power.' But he has sought concentration of political power to offset concentration of economic power. At the last, the two things become one, as Fascism proves."

10

ALADDIN'S LAMP

"BY THEIR fruits ye shall know them." American free enterprise is bearing fruit on many trees. With the exception of weapons of national defense, every single species is designed only to bring necessities, comforts, health and happiness to our people, and to the people of the entire world. Our free enterprise is doing infinitely more *good* to more people than all charitable organizations and governments put together, including the social welfare workers. It does that and in addition supports all charity, all education, all churches, and all government as part of the day's work.

A whole book ought to be devoted to the theme of the beneficent *purpose* of our free enterprise system. Its methods and some of its personnel have been seriously at fault. But a business system whose purpose is good, and achievements without precedent, ought not to be overthrown because of some faulty methods, especially when the methods of fascistic control are even more oppressive. The common sense of the matter is to improve the methods. And this is being done by the managers of business. The recent platform of the Congress of American Industry is one proof among many.

Meantime, in tens of thousands of shops, mines, offices, farms, laboratories, the lamps of Aladdin are being rubbed by modern genii, set free by the Constitution of the United

States, the barrier against Caesar.   There is the great
chemical industry marching with giant strides since the
end of the World War; there is the thrilling rush of the
iron horse as depicted at the New York World's Fair.
There is the drug, medical, surgical and dental supply industry; the electric utilities (an Aladdin's lamp in very
truth); chemurgy on the farm; the sanitary packing and
canning of meat, fish and food; the conquest of disease;
the Atlas of Steel, bearing a new world on his back; communications, radio, telephone and telegraph, shortening
the business day, bringing news, music, sports, plays and
public discussion into 27,500,000 homes, and extending
their friendly roofs over far distant relatives; electric re-
frigeration; air conditioning; the rapidly advancing art of
advertising; the silver screen where "all the world's a
stage." And naming these, you have just begun.

But a selection must be made. I happen to live in an
automobile town. In addition, during my eight years in
Congress, I became more familiar with the petroleum industry than with any other branch of our free enterprise.
So as a sample of free enterprise let me speak briefly of
these twin giants, petroleum and automobiles.

For other reasons they are a good selection. First: In
dollar volume motor vehicles and parts are No. 1, and
petroleum refining is No. 4 in the rank of our manufacturers. Second: They are among the least regimented
and the most free of any that might be named. Third:
Because they are a prime factor in such prosperity as we
enjoy, invigorating and sustaining scores of contributing
industries.

In passing it may be noted that the industries which
contributed most to recovery after the World War and
after 1932, have been the freest of governmental restraint; while those which have lagged in the prosperity
parade are those most regulated by the bureaucrats.

Apparently there is a law of economics at work here which indicates that Jefferson was and is still right, "That government is best which governs least."

But let us first consider the indictment that some government officials have drawn against the petroleum industry, its waste of oil and gas. There has been waste and it has been serious. And without doubt "Petroleum Pete" has been ruthless at times to get rich quick.

But *government has caused far more waste than industry*. That counter-charge will stand. It has come from the "rule of capture" laid down by the courts which are a part of government, and uncorrected by legislatures, which are a part of government.

It is probable that no decision by any court in the world's history, unless by some international tribunal, was ever so costly as the one that first legalized the "rule of capture" and set a precedent which other courts followed like sheep. In a word, this decision held that whoever brought petroleum to the surface of the ground became the owner of it, even though in so doing he drained oil that had formerly been under the surface of a neighboring land owner. Except for bloodshed, the Dred Scott decision was small change so far as loss of treasure is concerned. This decision forced the industry to be wasteful. It compelled every surface owner over an oil or gas pool to drill, regardless of price or market demand, in order to prevent his neighbor from draining his reserves—

"The good old rule, the simple plan,
  That he may take who has the power,
  And he shall keep who can."

Here was a matter peculiarly within the province of government. It was an impossible task for industry, owning thousands if not millions of separate tracts of land, to regulate. The state had the police power to act but did not.

But it is easy to be wise after the event. Seventy-five years ago who dreamed that the tiny acorn of rock oil would become the giant oak of a world industry? The courts followed the simple analogy of percolating underground waters—that whoever brought the hidden stream to the surface was entitled to it. What judge today, knowing only what men knew then, would have decided differently? The law has to grow, like everything else. And we have to pay for our education.

The only point in this is that there is a certain Pecksniffian hypocrisy in charging free enterprise for something which has been *the prime fault of government itself*. Apparently it is only in recent years that government has become impeccable, omniscient, heavenborn. But when petroleum was young the government brought shiploads of camels from Egypt to carry mail and military supplies across the Great Plains. But the American mule and jackass won that historic contest. The camel corps was disbanded and the bill charged to the taxpayers as is the usual custom.

But this is not the only defense the petroleum industry has to offer to the charge of waste. Leaders of the industry have been foremost in urging change in the law of capture, and in proposing other conservation measures. The result? Outside of two states, waste in drilling is negligible.

But the industry has done more. It has invested tens of millions of its own money in research to prevent waste, above or below ground. Let me mention one—cracking— a new method for refining gasoline from crude petroleum. In eighteen years, 1920–1938, the industry ran 15,633,-720,000 barrels of crude to the refining stills. From it, 6,143,216,000 barrels of gasoline were refined by cracking. If the cracking process had not been used 26,800,626,000 barrels of crude would have been necessary to produce the same amount of gasoline.

This means, in effect, that the industry saved or conserved by the cracking process 11,166,906,000 barrels of crude which otherwise would have been consumed to provide fuel for our motor transport. As the process has been constantly improved, today, by cracking, 52.42 per cent of every barrel of crude is saved.

Just what is 11,166,906,000 barrels of oil saved? From 1857–1938 the United States, producing 64 per cent of world's total produced 21,187,141,000 barrels of crude. So *in effect* the industry, in its research laboratories, has found more than half as much crude in eighteen years as has been brought out of the bowels of the earth in eighty years! Another way of stating it is that this practical saving has been twice as much as all oil produced in Texas —the Golconda of Black Gold—in its entire history! One test tube = two times Texas!

But do these National Socialists in Washington give the industry any credit for saving eleven billion barrels of oil? No. They do not. On the contrary they want leave of Congress to tell the industry how to run its affairs! A gentleman who admitted before my old committee that he had never seen an oil well before he entered the Cabinet, has now learned enough in his swivel chair at Washington to manage, not one oil company, but *all* companies!

Why, the industry, in its laboratories has saved more petroleum by six times than *the entire world used in 1937!* Let the Socialists chew on that for awhile.

And the way the government runs its own petroleum affairs on the lands of the public domain—well, I must refer you to a chapter in my book "Hot Oil," entitled "Uncle Sam, Landlord."

The next charge is that our reserves are melting away and only an allwise government can lengthen by two or three months the hour of complete exhaustion 50 or 100 or 500 years from now.

The answer is that the industry without any wisdom from Washington (D. C., not George!) has located and knows where to find more crude oil, still unused, than government officials or anybody else, estimated to be in the ground in 1915. That year the United States Geological Survey estimated there were 7,500,000,000 barrels of known reserves in the ground. The known amount on January 1, 1940, is 18,483,012,000 barrels, or over ten billion more. And by cracking the eighteen billion barrels will today produce more than five times as much gasoline as the 7.5 billions in 1915.

The Aladdin of free enterprise. In 1938, 145 drills went more than 10,000 feet below the earth's surface in search of oil, and one in Kern County, California, went 15,004 feet below, nearly three miles straight toward Hades, and found no oil at that depth! There's enterprise for you. Plugged back to 13,000 ft. it became a producer. These deep wells have cost up to a quarter of a million dollars each. A well 13,266 feet deep in Louisiana is a producer. The science and technology that has gone into metallurgy and other refinements necessary to send a bit down to explore these vast depths is in itself a romance worthy of the pen of Alexander Dumas. It's a sort of Pike's Peak or Bust standing on its head. For the drill has gone as deep as Pike's Peak is high (not from the surrounding plain but from sea level), with the Washington Monument and the Great Pyramid balanced on top. Imagine 12 Empire State Buildings built one on top of the other with an oil derrick surmounting them all, and from that vast height a well going down to the bedrock of Manhattan Island!

Well, what about the cost of gasoline? In January, 1939, the average United States price per gallon retail was .1876 cents, including tax. For a comparable amount, in Mr. Hitler's Berlin it was .596 cents, and in Mr. Mussolini's Rome it was .81 cents.

But 5.46 cents of that amount is tax. Without including the tax, gasoline in 1938 averaged 14.07 cents. In 1920, without tax, it averaged 29.74. So in 18 years, without any control from Washington the industry reduced gasoline to the retail consumer from nearly 30 cents to 14 cents. This has been a greater saving, by far, than in the all commodity index, and certainly a greater *saving* than our dear government has given us in taxes!

In 1938 the industry, in all its branches, paid government, federal, state and local, $1,286,114,473, for the privilege of being governed and for the use of tax built highways. In other words, the industry paid government 339 per cent more than its net earnings. Another example of government as a first preferred stock or lien holder in American business.

The great inventor, Michael Faraday, once was showing an invention to a bureaucrat. "What good is it?" demanded the Man of Government. "My lord," said Faraday, "it is something for you to tax." So with petroleum and motor vehicles. This tax total is equal to $9.89 per capita—man, woman and child. It would have maintained in 1936 all colleges and universities three times over. It is as much as all persons in Minnesota made in 1938, gross. It is more than one-third of the total operating income during 1938 of the railroads of the United States and more than three times their taxes. But that is the tax on petroleum and its allies only. All taxes on everybody in this country last year were equal to the *entire income* of all persons living west of the Mississippi River. If they had given government everything they raised, or made, or mined, or fished, and kept nothing, that would be it.

Wages and hours: In 1938 the petroleum industry employed 1,006,052 employes and paid its production and refining workers about $34 a week, or about 90 cents an hour

A BOOK THAT LIFTS THE SMOKE SCREEN

AROUND AMERICA'S FIFTH COLUMN

by SAMUEL B. PETTENGILL

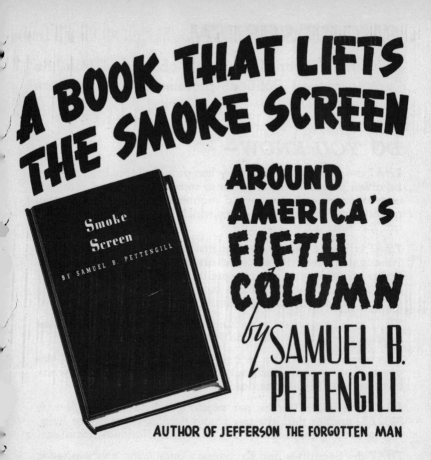

Smoke Screen
BY SAMUEL B. PETTENGILL

AUTHOR OF JEFFERSON THE FORGOTTEN MAN

Help Resell America in the American Market

"Here is Something to build on. The American people are not communists. The time and opportunity have come to all of us, but particularly to those in posts of responsibility and stewardship to resell America to Americans in the American Home Market. IT CAN BE DONE! All we need are a few salesmen with just a part of the spunk that lifted the words 'Washington', 'Jefferson' and 'Lincoln' out of the shadows."

—from the chapter "ARE WE LICKED"

SMOKE-SCREEN

Strips the veneer of "laudable objectives" from the "unguaranteed Political promises" of the "more abundant life."

DO YOU KNOW—

THAT the secretary of the Navy has proposed that the President be given power in peace times to seize factories and railroads and fix prices and wages and regiment labor—the same exact quantity and quality of power which Herr Hitler exercises to run the Nazi navy.

THAT a United States Senator has proposed that government "annuities" be sold — a clever and falsely labelled "humanitarian" device by which a spendthrift government would take over the assets of Insurance companies and undermine the security of some 64,000,000 thrifty people?

THAT a bill is actually pending to give the Secretary of the Interior power to manage the Petroleum Industry?

THAT another measure is before Congress to "socialize" the practice of medicine and thus destroy a great profession while lowering our health standards?

THAT the United States per capita public debt in 1938 was $432.65—greater than the per capita debt of Germany or Italy, where desperate peoples have turned to National Socialism!

THAT the Securities and Exchange Commission has warned a great utility company that it can't sell bonds, but must sell stock, thus taking the management away from those who own it—precisely as Hitler does across the sea!

THAT the Temporary National Economic Committee is reported to be preparing a "blast against American business beyond comparison with anything in history" — its thesis being that private enterprise is a failure; life insurance a blood-sucker; private banking outmoded—and that National Socialism is the hope of the world?

IT'S IN **SMOKE-SCREEN**

The book that blasts aggressively at the "Silent Erosion of Free Enterprise"

"ARE WE LICKED?"

SMOKE-SCREEN has the answer and smashes all defeatist argument . . .

The "mass-man" can be appealed to, and once aroused and informed, his judgement is safe and dependable.

He goes to the movies, says PETTENGILL — "and don't the 'good movies' invariably draw the crowds—Look at the advertisements. Who are they written for—billboard, street car, magazine and newspaper? The 'mass-man'. Business men in their advertising copy 'play up' to the 'mass-man', and find that *it pays!"*

The *MASS-MAN* wants and demands the *BEST*, not the *WORST*. FORTUNE MAGAZINE in its poll printed March, 1940 shows that even the poorest American believes in the Constitution of the United States; believes in private ownership of property and the profit motive; believes that investors are entitled to fair treatment; believes the law should place no limit to the reward of honest achievement. SUCH IS THE AMERICAN CREED.

———

PETTENGILL Writes for the great Middle Class and out of an authoritative background that includes eight years in the Congress of the United States and a wealth of contacts embracing men and events of national significance.

Author of JEFFERSON THE FORGOTTEN MAN, in its third edition, and one of the most remarkable books of the decade, and nationally quoted by reason of his column "THE GENTLEMAN FROM INDIANA" appearing in sixty daily papers from coast to coast, Samuel B. Pettengill is ably equipped. You'll agree with him that "WE'RE NOT LICKED" when you read —

SMOKE-SCREEN

CREEPING COLLECTIVISM

From SMOKE-SCREEN — *"But so silently has this Nazification of America gone on that there are many good and patriotic people who think 'you are seeing things under the bed' if you tell them we are on the German road. Is life insurance to be next?"*

You Can Help Effectively

The first job is to inform and arouse 250,000 men and women in position to give leadership — editors, physicians, clergymen, lawyers, business men, large and small, heads of women, labor and farm organizations.

With Their Help and Yours, The Country Can Be Aroused

Help place a copy of SMOKE-SCREEN in their hands. This is your fight for your own and your children's greatest heritage — Constitutional Democracy and the American System of Free Enterprise.

DISTRIBUTE SMOKE-SCREEN

Make copies available to others. Books will be sent postpaid to addresses you furnish; have them placed in your Public Library, in schools, colleges, among leaders in your community and among friends and business acquaintances.

OFFERED IN ATTRACTIVE SPECIAL EDITION

	1 copy postpaid anywhere . . .	$1.00
2 to	5 copies postpaid anywhere . .	80¢ each
6 to	10 copies postpaid anywhere . .	75¢ each
11 to	50 copies postpaid anywhere . .	70¢ each
51 to	100 copies postpaid anywhere . .	65¢ each
101 or more copies postpaid anywhere .	60¢ each

Send your order to

AMERICA'S FUTURE • INC.

A Non-profit Educational Organization

205 EAST 42nd STREET   NEW YORK, N. Y.

for an average of about 37 hours per week—one of the highest wage scales in America. Only 2 workers in 100 quit, or were discharged or laid off.

Nor has the industry been careless of the lives or limbs of its workers. It sustained less than 13 disabling injuries per 1,000,000 man hours worked. In severity, the worker lost only one day's work in 72 eight hour days, or one day in over 15 weeks, and most of these injuries were of a minor character.

The accident record in the automobile industry was even better—7.66 injuries in 1,000,000 man-hours worked, and only one day lost in 164 eight-hour days, or one day in over seven months.

The record in the automobile industry parallels petroleum. It, too, pays heavy taxes, receives no subsidies or gifts from government, asks little but freedom to plan and perform, is constantly selling a better and better car at a low price for a very low margin of profit and pays high wages for a shortening week's work. The makers of the four or five popular-priced cars average no more than $29 per car, and of this amount one-third to one-half is profit derived from the sale of accessories and replacements.

There are now about 30,000,000 registered automobiles and trucks in the United States, 68 per cent of world total. Americans have one motor vehicle to four persons; Germany one to 42 persons; Italy one to 93 and Russia sayeth not. No record.

To manufacture these cars and equipment $1,300,652,-000 is invested in plants employing directly in a good year, like 1937, 517,000 workers. It is estimated that directly and indirectly the automobile and petroleum industries are responsible for 6,500,000 being at work in production, distribution, road building, servicing and driving. The motor vehicles—car, truck, bus and tractor—take 90 per cent of all gasoline, 80 per cent of rubber, 69 per cent of plate glass, 51 per cent of strip steel, 53 per cent of malleable iron, 40 per cent of mohair, 29 per cent of nickel, 35 per cent of all lead consumed in America, to say nothing of cotton, leather, copper, aluminum, zinc, lumber, etc. The automobile industry is even a huge buyer of soy beans, turpentine, wool, sugar, cane, corn, flax seed and the "little busy bee employs each shining hour" to produce 19 tons of beeswax annually for automobiles.

These 30,000,000 motor vehicles average 8,870 miles yearly, or 266 billion miles—enough to go to the moon and back nearly 554,000 times! A round trip of 480,000 miles!

In 1920 we produced 2,227,349 cars and trucks that sold at average retail price of $1,336. In 1937 this giant of free enterprise produced 5,016,437 cars and trucks which sold at an average of $789—and a far better car, in looks, performance, comfort and safety for $547 less.

If these 5,016,437 vehicles had sold at the same price that prevailed in 1920 the cost would have been $2,743,-991,039 more. That saving, plus a better car, was passed on in 1937 to these 5,000,000 buyers. In short the industry, without any prodding from government, gave the buyer a better car, and by cost comparison, $547 to spend on other things. In other words, in 1920 the buyer would have had to spend $1,336, retail cost, for a car alone. To-day he can buy a better car for $789, retail cost, and keep or spend the difference of $547. This released $547 to him as a buying market for other commodities, increasing employment elsewhere in an ever-widening circle, or he could save it as a nest egg for a rainy day.

Not only has free enterprise given the American buyer a constantly better car with cheaper and less frequent repairs, but better gasoline to drive it, better oil to lubricate it, better and safer tires to cushion it, and better and safer roads to drive it on.

All this has resulted in enormous savings to the American people. In 1920 the cost of owning and operating the popular four-door passenger automobiles, including depreciation against original purchase price, was 7.4 cents per mile per car. In 1938 it was 4.3 cents per mile per car. Three and one-tenths cents saved seems a tiny sum—so small that it might even escape the attention of a careless Scotsman!

But, multiplied by 266,000,000,000 miles for all cars driven in a single year in America, it amounts to a saving of $11,438,000,000! That is the equivalent of a total annual wage raise of over $11,000,000,000 which is shared by everyone who drives a car. This is what research and free enterprise have done for American people in 18 years, in automobile transportation alone, in its ceaseless effort to produce better for less.

Of course, if these huge savings in the cost of owning and driving an automobile had not been made, 5,016,437 cars would not have been sold in 1937, nor would 30,000,000 be driving today. But this is only another way of proving what free enterprise has done. And yet millions of people today continue to believe that the machine is the enemy of mankind.

When we compare what free enterprise has done to lower the cost of living and improve the standard of living, with what the politicians have done, and at what cost, National Socialism burns with a feebler light.

The petroleum and automobile industries, as well as industry generally, are opposed to the concentration of all political and economic power at Washington. That is to say, they are opposed to changing our form of government. They want to continue as parts of the competitive free enterprise system engaging in a ceaseless struggle for the consumer's good will by offering most and best for least.

But, fearing a strangling fascistic control of industry by government, they have not sought to run wild from all reasonable policing of their business. The petroleum industry has given its great backing to interstate compacts for necessary regulation, as an alternative to federal centralization of power and the destruction of the rights and duties of the States of the Union.

And, in similar fashion, the automobile industry, as an alternative to National Socialism, has gotten strongly behind uniform state legislation with respect to highway safety and responsibility. For example, the uniform Motor Vehicle Code consists of five acts:

1. Regulation, Certificate of Title and Anti-Theft Act.
2. Operators and Chauffeurs License Act.
3. Civil Liability Act.
4. Safety Responsibility Act.
5. Regulating Traffic on Highways.

Every state in the United States already has adopted some part of this model legislation. 44 have adopted the License Act, 26 the Civil Liability Act, 37 the Traffic Regulations Act.

In addition, a model city ordinance has been adopted by scores of cities and towns, large and small, in every section of the country.

As a result of these efforts to reduce accident ratios, motor vehicle traffic fatalities, per 100,000,000 vehicle miles has declined from 17.7 in 1927 to 12.9 in 1938. 1938 safety record improved 18 per cent over 1937, a condition reflected in every state in the Union but three.

So, when the fair minded American jury of 130,000,000 people read articles written in pink ink attacking business as having no "social conscience," these bits of evidence are offered by counsel for the defense.

To summarize: If they had to, these 130,000,000 Americans could all get into these 30,000,000 cars and all ride on rubber at the same instant of time—*a nation on wheels!* When Hitler, or Stalin, or Mussolini do half as much, it will be twice as much as they have done!

11

GUINEA PIG—1940 MODEL

AMERICA IS still a great country. Its unused strength is enormous. No depression or war in its history has yet broken its spirit. It seems plain that certain government brakes must be released before we can regain our old forward stride and earn the $90 or $100 billion dollar income of which we are inherently capable. Otherwise we look ahead to a halting recovery financed by constant additions to the debt until we have "exhausted the deficit." Then what?

It may be that nothing yet done has finally determined our fate. It is probable that the *direction* we are going and the continuity of our march is more important than the distance so far travelled.

If we can stop!

Many will say that we have not yet gone National Socialist, and may approve our course thus far. But even these must admit that we cannot continue long in the present *direction* without coming late or soon to National Socialism.

It may be that we can go on half socialist and half free. It may be that in time we will be able to digest federal control of banking, credit, railroads, shipping, bituminous coal, radio, utilities, gold, silver, investment, farming, labor relations, wages, hours, etc., and still remain free citizens reading free newspapers, listening to a free radio, going to a free church, our children in free schools, and casting a free man's vote on election day. I would regard this as doubtful and the price in a lower standard of living both certain and large.

But whatever margin of freedom we yet have, it seems rash indeed to permit it to be further whittled away. Nevertheless that is proposed. Pending are bills to federalize education, to start toward state medicine, to control investment trusts, to tax machinery and strangle mechanical progress, to require *all* corporations in interstate commerce to be chartered and controlled by Washington—the Industrial Mobilization Plan, a completely fascistic scheme—many others.

But having selected automobiles and petroleum as models of free enterprise, let us inquire what our New Deal National Socialists propose to do to them.

Congressman Patman of Texas has worked out "a motor vehicle industry act," whereby a new federal bureaucracy would undertake to control the contracts between manufacturers and dealers, prevent new men entering the dealer field (as the Nazis tell who can do what), thus giving dealers already in business a monopoly, fix trade-in allowances for used cars, etc. This in time would probably lead to government price fixing of new cars. For when the price of the finished product is determined by bureaucrats they must then move in the direction of fixing all cost elements that make up that price—not only margin of profits to the industry, but wages to the worker, as today in Germany, to say nothing of deciding what companies may make cars, and how many cars to each company.[1]

---

[1] "The Nazis began by regulating the sale of grain—first wheat and rye, then also of oats and barley. Then they decided not only upon minimum prices but upon fixed prices, with variations for region and season. From then on every producer has not only the right but also the duty of bringing into the market a fixed quantity of products at fixed

So far we have sugar coated this by calling it "planned economy." But when the sugar coating is off there is nothing left but the bitter taste of Naziism, Fascism or Communism.

In the petroleum industry a bill is pending which was introduced by Congressman William P. Cole, Jr., of Maryland. It is known as the Cole bill although it was written by Secretary Ickes' staff and Congressman Cole has stated that he by no means approves the bill as written.

This bill, if enacted, will give the Secretary of the Interior not only final absolute power to prescribe all means and methods by which petroleum is produced, e.g., how many and how far apart every well shall be drilled and who may drill them, but also the power to determine for what purposes petroleum and all of its products may be used. For example, he could prescribe what proportion of the product may be used for gasoline, fuel oil, and any other of the hundreds of petroleum derivatives. In granting him this power, the bill would relegate to the background the authority of all state governments to deal with the subject matter.

Let us see where this bill would start, and where, by the implacable Nemesis that pursues programs of this kidney, it would probably end.

In 1934 another petroleum bill was before Congress known as the Thomas-Disney bill. Although at that time certain elements in the industry favored its passage, it never got on the House calendar as a result of decisions made by Mr. Cole and his subcommittee colleagues, of whom I was one. Instead support was given to interstate

times. All the intermediaries between the producer and the consumer, the grain merchants, the millers, the flour dealers, the bakers, etc., are likewise forced to observe the fixed prices and to sell fixed quantities of productions for consumption." From The Third Reich, by Henry Lichtenberger.

compacts among the oil producing states whereby they undertook to retain states' rights and perform states' duties! As they should!

Today the petroleum industry is united almost to a man against the pending bill. But that is not the only strange thing to be noticed. In 1934 not a single governor ventured to oppose the Thomas-Disney bill, and two, Marland of Oklahoma and Landon of Kansas, gave it a tearful blessing. Today twelve governors, eight in person, and four by personal representatives, have appeared before Mr. Cole's committee in Washington in protest against *any more* federal control over industries or states. "Don't give us any more don'ts," said Governor Ayres of Montana. Other states making official protest by governor or other representatives were Wyoming, Colorado, New Mexico, Kansas, Oklahoma, Texas, Arkansas, Michigan, Pennsylvania, West Virginia, Georgia, Louisiana and Mississippi, 14 in all.

When it is considered that the majority of these governors were Democrats who had decided to fight for the century-long tradition of states' rights, and thus picked up the gauge of battle against New Deal socialism, it becomes a political sign of the utmost significance. Governor Phillips of Oklahoma told the Congressmen, "Your conclusions in this matter may not only affect a great industry but may fashion and shape the destiny of the nation." And Governor Ratner of Kansas added, "This bill is a step which would undermine the basic structure of the Republic."

Why did these men not only feel this way, but do a thing without precedent in seven years—come all the way to Washington to say so in public? What induced them to reexamine the ancient foundations of the Republic and conclude they were still sound and strong? "Don't do to petroleum what you have done to the railroads," said one

("decree" is the word used in Germany) of the Secretary of the Interior, or his appointed agent.

It goes far beyond that or any New Deal act now, to my knowledge, on the statute books. It prohibits the production of a spoonful of petroleum in any well in any state which the Secretary may find to be "wasteful." It forbids anyone to drill a well on his own property if the Secretary forbids. It would subject to fine and imprisonment the forbidden production by a farmer of natural gas to heat his own home. A state school or university on state owned land could not, if the Secretary forbade, pipe from its own gas wells.

Moreover, it appears to control not only production, however local, but use, however local. Under the bill the Secretary or his agent could say that crude oil should not be used for fuel oil. And in the light of the fact that Mr. John L. Lewis wants to place a penalty tax on fuel oil in order to compel people to buy coal, this control over the use of petroleum is something to be thought of if Mr. Lewis or anyone like him, such as Toledano in Mexico, ever controls the federal government. We would then subject petroleum to inter-industry rackets for the benefit of those close to the throne.

Now it must be plain that if this petroleum bill becomes a precedent for the extension of federal power, there is not a single national resource which cannot be brought within the federal orbit. If the Secretary of the Interior can decide who shall and who shall not drill wells for petroleum or natural gas, then with equal logic (national defense is the new smoke-screen) he can control the production of every mine and every ton of coal, coke, iron ore, lead, zinc, copper, silver, gold, bauxite, aluminum, feldspar, Fuller's earth, gypsum, lime, magnesium, manganese, phosphate, salt, sand and gravel, slate, marble, granite, limestone, sulphur, tin, and all other minerals. For petroleum is a mineral.

It seems, too, that the theory of this bill would also with equal constitutional logic (sic) give the federal government control of the use of the water in every stream and river, and the growth and cutting of all timber, as is requested by the Forestry Service.

I realize that the thesis of this book, that we are moving toward a Nazi America, must be startling to readers who have had neither time, nor opportunity to attempt to keep pace with the revolutionary ideas flooding the Nation's capitol city, and particularly "downtown" Washington. But if anyone will take the time to read this, and other bills, and then read the story of German industry and commerce and agriculture since January, 1933, when Hitler came to power, I ask him in all candor to point out what greater power, if any, Hitler has over Nazi industry than is proposed to be given to bureaucrats in Washington.

Although this chapter has dealt chiefly with petroleum, with which I am most familiar, it uses petroleum as an example for all industry. Heretofore one industry after another has been foolish enough to stand mute as they watch their neighbors being thrown to the crocodile on the theory that as long as it is done, the crocodile won't bite *them*. But when all the neighbors are gone, what will the crocodile do then?

The time has come, I respectfully submit from this record, when *all* American industries *must join forces* to protect each other, as the bull bison on the western plains formed a common ring with their fighting tools forward and their tails up, and their cows and calves inside, when the wolves came down from the timber.

Governor Carl E. Bailey, Democrat, of Arkansas, stated the issue: "I would rather that my state be without petroleum than that *we should lose our form of government.*"

And as Chief Justice Charles Evans Hughes said, in Carter v. Carter Coal Co., 298 U.S. 56 (1936), and in the more recent case of Santa Cruz Fruit Co. v. National Labor Relations Board, 303 U.S. 453 (1938),

"the power to regulate commerce among the several states is not power to regulate industry within the state"; and "this principle is *essential to the maintenance of our constitutional system.*"

This conclusion was not only implicit in the hearts of the men who wrote the Constitution in 1787 but, it has been restated again and again by courts, presidents, public officials, editors and party platforms of both parties and *particularly* by the Democratic party, the historic opponent against "compounding the people into one common mass."

What is involved, therefore, is not the fate of automobiles, or petroleum, or coal, etc., as such. What is at stake today is the "maintenance of our constitutional system."

The Constitution and New Deal Socialism cannot permanently co-exist on American soil. The friends of our form of government in both great parties must halt this onward march toward a Nazi America, or by a creeping paralysis concealed from the patient it will result in the death of the Republic.

* * * * * * *

"Two weeks after the March (1933) elections, Adolf Hitler served notice in the Garrison Church of Potsdam, where Frederick the Great lies buried: 'In spite of their traditions, the independent lives of the scattered German States are not only useless, but disastrous for the prestige and welfare of our nation.' These words were followed by the law that I have already mentioned.

"Since the expression of criticism on any governmental act is impossible, it would be difficult to ascertain how the majority of Germans like the new arrangement. For a more definite appraisal of the States' attitude toward the change, one will have to wait for Germany's liberation from the Hitler terror.

"A long chapter of Germany's history ended with the promulgation of the 'Law for the Uniformity of the States with the Reich' in the late spring of 1933. It was an important move in the transformation of the Federal Reich into a single centralized State.

"It was as if the Federal government in Washington had abolished the sovereignty of the forty-eight States of this country by dismissing their governors and putting in charge of them appointees responsible only to the President.

"Prussia, Bavaria, Saxony—to mention only the most outstanding of the seventeen German States—became scarcely more than geographic designations.

"Young Nazis burning the State line markers, merely imitated what the halbardiers of the French King had done centuries ago.

"The Nazi reorganization of the Reich is a revolutionary break with the past, with ancient traditions, and with national sentiments. It is, however, in keeping with the National Socialist policy to establish a 'totalitarian' State in which there is only one God, Germany, and only one prophet, Adolf Hitler.

"This policy demands the unification of the Reich both physically and spiritually—an autocratic country, bending to the will of the Leader. The individual States must be abolished because their existence spells the danger of rival loyalties, eclipsing the only true faith. Political and spiritual resistance must be made impossible. Every function of the State must be coordinated.

"Under the Law of the Uniformity of the States with the Reich, the central government in Berlin, acting through the President, appointed Vice-Regents for each of the seventeen States. The Vice-Regents were made responsible only to the Federal government, and they could not be overthrown by a vote of 'no-confidence' of the State legislatures.

"They were empowered to appoint the State governments, which were responsible to them and not to their States. Both the legislatures and the governments were threatened with being put out of business in the near future and then the map would be clean of German States. Meanwhile the legislatures and governments were allowed to lead a shadow existence, stripped of the right to voice opinions or to command.

"Celebrating the first anniversary of the Nazi rule on January 30, 1934, the Reichstag adopted in five minutes the Reich Reform Bill, permanently abolishing the State Legislatures and placing their governments under the direct authority of Berlin, of which they will be merely the executive local organs."—From Chapter "The Twilight of the German Free States" in "The New Deal in Europe" by Emil Lengyel.

12

ARE WE LICKED?

THERE IS a defeatist attitude in the air. In my judgment it is wholly unjustified.

The finest thing ever said about General Grant was by President Coolidge, "He did not waste his time trying to find substitutes for victory."

Let us take this defeatist philosophy apart and see what makes it tick. It comes from such books as "The Decline of the West" by Spengler, and "The Revolt of the Masses" by Ortega y Gasset, which have been used by our sterile intellectuals (in the business world particularly) as an excuse for their own political laziness. The thesis is that the "mass-man" is in charge, that he is half-gorilla, happy only when trampling civilization under foot. It is supposed that he is the easy prey of demagogues, that he is incapable of discrimination, and so, "when this dumb terror shall rise to judge the world," quoting from Edwin Markham's "The Man With the Hoe," we abjectly confess our doom.

This stuff makes me ill. The "mass-man" has been around a long time. He followed Jefferson. He was at Valley Forge. He voted for Lincoln. He rode behind Robert E. Lee. "Father Abraham" knew the color of his eyes. He was just one of the "plain people" to him.

Yes, it was the "mass-man" who fought the French and American Revolutions—and followed Mazzini and Garibaldi, and Bolivar, and Hampden, and Robert Emmet and William Tell, and Robert, the Bruce, and Martin Luther and John Wesley, and George Whitefield and Dwight L. Moody, and John Bunyan and Jacques Bossuet, and Pierre Abelard and Pere Marquette. Yes, and weren't there a lot of "mass-men" around the Man of Galilee? They "heard him gladly," I once read.

Where did all these great men get the sinews of their strength? Who knelt when St. Bernard preached the crusades? Were they the manicured dilettantes of defeat? Who listened when St. Augustine in the year 400 said "For many have been tried even with hunger and rags, *and have been found gold,* and have not been forsaken by God"? It was the "mass-man" who listened, more ignorant, more illiterate, more hungry, more hopeless and more exploited than his brother today. They were the "great unwashed." There was no soap. But that fact did not prevent them from being our ancestors.

The trouble now is not the "mass-man." The trouble is that his natural leaders have sheathed their swords, hung their tails between their legs, and deserted the colors. The "mass-man" is just as avid for leaders *he can trust* as he has ever been. There is complete sincerity in his eyes. "Show us the way out. Give it to us straight. How can we save our shirts? How can we leave our children a better chance?" These are the things they ask, and if from time to time they follow charlatans like Huey Long, whose fault is it, in Heaven's name? Yes, they have been "plundered, profaned and disinherited," again and again. Yes, they have bought plenty of gold bricks from political fakirs. But even when they do, is there not something creditable about it? Is it not that they *want* something *better* than they have, not something *worse?*

And if they revolt against exploitation, as they did in 1776, or 1793, or in recent years, whether it is the tyranny of capital, or labor, or soldier, or politician or priest, I salute them. At times they have been cruel and callous as in the Terror of '93, when they sent many innocents to the guillotine. But I have never forgotten a line in Les Miserables, "I will weep for you over the children of kings, if you will weep with me over the children of the people."

No. I'm not here to canonize the "mass-man." He has his vices, aplenty. But he is the raw material of *all the civilization there is,* or *ever was,* or *ever will be.*

We have been too easy in swallowing this dogma of decadence and defeat. We are daily surrounded by facts that prove it a fantasy. The "mass-man" certainly goes to the movies. And don't the "good" movies draw the crowds —The Covered Wagon, David Copperfield, Little Women, The Birth of a Nation, Captains Courageous, Gone With the Wind? Look at the advertisements. Who are they written for—billboard, street car, magazine, newspaper? The "mass-man." Do poor taste ads sell goods, whether automobiles, cigarettes, or homes? Do our business men, in their advertising, play *down* to the "mass-man"? No, they play *up,* and find that it *pays.* Did you ever know the father or mother of the poorest child who didn't want the *best* in schools?

No, this "mass-man" wants the *best,* not the *worst.* The thought you hear expressed in Pullman cars that he has no use for bathtubs except to use them for coal scuttles is sheer bunk. Ask Crane, ask Kohler.

I am satisfied, too, that this "mass-man" wants the *best government,* also. Fortune Magazine of March, 1940, says that its poll shows that even the poorest American believes in the Constitution of the United States; believes in the private ownership of property and the profit motive; believes that investors are entitled to fair treatment; believes the law should place no limit to the reward of honest achievement. Such is the American creed.

Here is something to build on. The American people are not communists. The time and opportunity have come to all of us, but particularly to those in posts of responsibility and stewardship, to resell America to Americans in the American home market. It can be done. All we need are a few salesmen with just a part of the spunk that lifted the words "Washington," "Jefferson" and "Lincoln" out of the shadows.

13

POST SCRIPT FOR ACTION

IN THIS special printing of "Smoke-Screen," the National Committee to Uphold Constitutional Government has suggested that I ought to answer some of the questions implied in "Are We Licked"? In other words, what can the average citizen do to preserve constitutional government and our system of free enterprise?

There are many things he can do in his capacity as a citizen of his home community and of his state as well as a citizen of the nation.

In my judgment, however, the most important single thing he can do is to send *strong men* to Congress.

By that I mean Senators and Representatives of character, courage, and loyalty to free institutions.

This effort should be wholly nonpartisan. The real division today is not between the Democratic and Republican parties as history knows them. It is between the men and women in both great parties on the one hand who believe in the free institutions which have made this the greatest nation in the world; and on the other hand those who are willing to confess that our great effort to be free has failed and we must now submit our fate to a government which, whatever its name or label, will be a species of National Socialism.

It is an issue upon which Democrats and Republicans can stand together and *must* stand together if what Abraham Lincoln called "this last best hope of earth" is to be the legacy of our children.

The election of strong men to House and Senate this year is, of course, of extraordinary importance, but two years from now and four years from now, and thereafter, the importance will not be less.

In the face of the totalitarian tide that is now sweeping over a war-mad world, the necessity, "that this Nation under God shall have a new birth of freedom" is greater today than it was then. That need is probably greater today than it was even when Washington lived.

If we are to have this new birth of freedom we must strengthen the Congress of the United States. We should retain in Congress those Senators and Representatives, both Republican and Democrat, who have demonstrated under fire their loyalty to fundamental principles and the courage to defend them. We have an especial obligation to those who made a brave fight for the independence of Congress and the independence of the courts.

While retaining these men we should replace those Senators and Representatives who have not demonstrated this loyalty nor this courage.

We cannot disregard the human factor in government. All government is necessarily administered by MEN. The strength of free institutions depends upon the strength of the MEN who administer free institutions.

The necessity for a strong Congress is greater today than it has ever been, for two reasons at least:

First, because the Supreme Court of the United States is no longer a predictable body.

Second, Supreme Court decisions already made in effect vest in Congress tremendous powers that heretofore we had not thought Congress possessed. What has occurred in the past few years has been in effect the equivalent of an amendment of the Constitution of the United States by judicial interpretation of the most far reaching consequence.

The greater the power, the greater the necessity that it be exercised wisely and courageously, in the same way that the selection of a general to command an army is more important than that of a sergeant to command a platoon.

At the present time the attention of the nation is largely and somewhat hysterically centered upon the question of who will be nominated and elected President of the United States during the next four years. But the nomination and election of a President is not going to pay the national debt. It is not automatically going to cure unemployment either of idle dollars or idle men. It is not going to balance the budget. It is not going to stop deficits. It will not reduce taxes. It will not prevent the threat some day in the future of inflation, repudiation or national bankruptcy. It may not keep us out of war.

Any man who is President of the United States by virtue of his commanding position may greatly aid in these matters, but he cannot accomplish them. If legislation is wise there is a good chance it will be wisely administered, but if the legislation is bad, even the best administration cannot cure the evil.

With a strong Congress an ambitious President can do little harm, and with a weak Congress a strong President can do little good.

The judiciary can interpret only such laws as Congress enacts and the executive can administer only such laws as Congress enacts. Congress is the *originating* body both in legislation, taxation and the appropriation of public funds.

The fact is that your beliefs can be translated into political action far more effectively by your vote for Congressman and Senator than for President of the United

States. In the average Congressional district about 100,-000 votes are cast in the fall election, and 50,000 in the primary election. But for President of the United States about 45,000,000 votes are cast. Your vote, therefore, for Congressman in the fall election is about 450 times as important as your vote for President, and your vote in a primary election for Congressman is about 900 times as important as your vote for President. A change of five votes in a hundred generally elects or defeats a candidate for Congress. You can be one of the five.

There is another point I wish to call to your attention. Many people seem to think that in a body as large as Congress—435 members of the House, 96 in the Senate, 531 in all—that the vote of the individual Congressman or Senator is submerged by the number. What people do not sufficiently realize is that the work of Congress is chiefly done by its committees. For example, the House of Representatives is divided into 44 committees to which all legislation is referred. These committees consist of from 7 or 9 up to 25 members. Legislation is first considered in committee. It is there rewritten. It is the *committee* that determines whether bills should be reported favorably or not. In the smaller group of the congressional committee the importance of even one strong Congressman increases greatly.

In short, all legislation goes through the bottle necks of congressional committees. The personnel of these committees is therefore of vital importance. What the committees do, Congress generally does. Although bills are modified on the floor of the House and Senate, nevertheless it is a fair statement to say that what happens on the floor of the House or Senate is in effect a ratification or rejection of what the committee has done.

This can be illustrated by the struggle over the bill to pack the Supreme Court of the United States. That was referred to the Senate Committee of the Judiciary of 18 members. That bill met its death blow by the adverse report of that committee of 10 to 8; in other words, a change of *two votes* would have changed the result. It was fortunate for the republic that there were enough strong men on that particular committee.

This case which I have used as an illustration could be repeated over and over with respect to one important bill after another. I could point out from historical facts how the presence or absence of *one or two strong men* on a congressional committee has changed the whole course of legislation.

But not only in the Committees, but in the whole body of Congress, *men*—not rubber stamps—are important. On the floor, it is often the case that the result is determined by a very few men giving not only votes but *leadership* to one side or the other. For example, in 1938, the Executive Reorganization Bill was defeated in the House by a margin of only 11 votes, where a change of six votes in over 400 would have changed the result.

Without making a false hero of anyone, the fact remains that the legislative branch is the heart of free institutions. Freedom has always risen or declined with the strength or weakness of the legislative body. It can be safely stated that no legislature ever destroyed the liberty of its constituents *so long as it retained the powers given it by them*. As Thomas Jefferson said, "The authority of Congress can never be weakened without injury to the Union." We have seen this proved in the last few years.